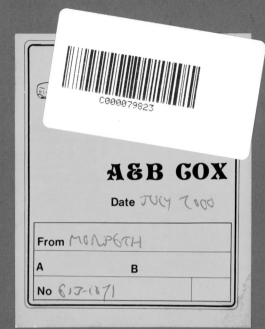

A&B COX

Date JULY 2000

From MORPETH	
A	B
No 817-1871	

Nesting Birds of the Coastal Islands

Number Twenty-Two
The Corrie Herring Hooks Series

Text and Photography by John C. Dyes

Nesting Birds of the Coastal Islands

A
NATURALIST'S
YEAR ON
GALVESTON
BAY

 UNIVERSITY OF TEXAS PRESS, AUSTIN

Frontispiece:
The Snowy Egret in
the foreground shows off
its breeding plumage
while its mate in the
background preens
itself.

Requests for permission to reproduce material from this work should be sent to Permissions, University of Texas Press, Box 7819, Austin, TX 78713-7819.

∞The paper used in this publication meets the minimum requirements of American National Standard for Information Sciences—Permanence of Paper for Printed Library Materials, ANSI Z39.48-1984.

Library of Congress Cataloging-in-Publication Data

Dyes, John C. (John Clifton), date
   Nesting birds of the coastal islands : a naturalist's year on Galveston Bay / text and photography by John C. Dyes. — 1st ed.
     p.   cm. — (The Corrie Herring Hooks series ; no. 22)
   Includes bibliographical references and index.
   ISBN 0-292-71567-6 (alk. paper)
    1. Ciconiiformes—Texas—Galveston Bay—Nests. 2. Ciconiiformes—Texas—Laguna Madre—Nests. 3. Charadriiformes—Texas—Galveston Bay—Nests. 4. Charadriiformes—Texas—Laguna Madre—Nests. 5. Barrier Islands—Texas. 6. Ciconiiformes—Texas—Galveston Bay—Nests—Pictorial works. 7. Ciconiiformes—Texas—Laguna Madre—Nests—Pictorial works. 8. Charadriiformes—Texas—Galveston Bay—Nests—Pictorial works. 9. Charadriiformes—Texas—Laguna Madre—Nests—Pictorial works. I. Title. II. Series.
QL696.C5D94   1993
598'.34'09764139—dc20   92-29457

TO MY WIFE,
ALLENA,
WHO BELIEVED
IN THIS
PROJECT

Contents

Preface

In this book I follow twenty-two species of colonial wading birds, gulls, and terns through a one-year nesting cycle. The term "colonial" is used for birds that nest in groups ranging from a half-dozen to tens of thousands or more. Ornithologists are not sure whether the prime reason for gathering in the large colonies is to pass information on to the young birds or to find safety from predators. Both theories may be correct. Herons feed alone, Roseate Spoonbills feed in flocks, but the young of both may rely on the adults to show them where and how to feed. The "safety from predator" theory may also be true since the colonial birds return yearly to the islands with no predator problems.

This group of birds caught my interest for a combination of reasons. I have been an out-of-doors person all my life and have been photographing nature for more than thirty years. I was a chemical engineer and worked in a refinery for many years, but consider myself to be an active environmentalist and am a member of the National Audubon Society, the Sierra Club, and the Nature Conservancy. I love birds in general but am color blind and have difficulty identifying many perching birds. However, the wading birds, gulls, and terns are no problem. And, perhaps through my Viking ancestry, I inherited a love

Opposite page: The young Laughing Gull, in its nest on Little Pelican Island, feels very secure protected by the surrounding grasses.

of salt water and everything associated with it. I was introduced to the colonial birds by Elric McHenry, one of the Houston area's top birders, when he asked if I wanted to take part in the annual Texas Colonial Waterbird Census conducted by the Texas Waterbird Society. Since I had a boat, I could provide transportation to the islands in the southern part of Galveston Bay where we were to conduct our survey. I was simply bowled over when I saw the amount of nesting right in my local area and started going back on my own to photograph. With this introduction and the combination of factors in my background, this book project clicked into place. All the nesting is on islands, so I use a 20-foot lightweight, shallow-draft boat for transportation.

The observations and photographs were made in the Galveston Bay and Laguna Madre areas over an eight-year period and then, for the purposes of this book, condensed into a one-year period. Although the photographs were taken within a rather limited geographical range, the birds being photographed have much wider ranges. Some, like the Reddish Egret, breed only on the Gulf Coast south to Central America, while others, like the Great Egret, breed worldwide.

On the Texas coast the birds have an extended nesting period, but their season is like a bell-shaped curve. The birds' nesting year starts in February, builds during March and April, reaches a crescendo around the first of June, then declines rapidly to end, for all practical purposes, in July. A few stragglers may still be around in August and September. In the warm southern rookeries there is a great deal of overlap within species. For instance, one group of White Ibis may start nesting in March and have their young raised by June while elsewhere another group will be starting nests in June.

Since no one island in the Galveston Bay area supports all the birds covered in this book, I photographed on eight different islands, some of which are natural. Others are spoil islands, that is, human-made islands that were built from materials dredged up during the building of the Intracoastal Waterway and other ship and barge channels. Human-made islands have been the birds' salvation. Several of the birds, like the Least Terns and Black Skimmers, once nested on the beaches. When people, with their automobiles, children, dogs, and cats, discovered the beaches, the birds were forced to move to the islands. Also, there were at one time large inland heron and egret rookeries, but most have been developed out of existence, forcing these birds onto the islands. For the most part, the islands provide excellent nesting habitat near good feeding grounds. Of all the nesting islands in the Galveston Bay area, only three, North Deer, Rollover Pass, and Vingt-et-un are National Audubon Society (NAS) sanctuaries where wardens keep a daily watch to protect the birds from sightseers.

Due to budget constraints in the past, the colonial wading birds have received little active attention from the Texas Parks and Wildlife Department. But, at this writing, the TPWD is expanding its nongame species programs. It is developing plans to identify rookery areas, improving habitat to maintain species diversity, and removing predators from nesting sites, in an effort to manage twenty-five species of colonial water birds in Texas. Funds have been allocated to monitor Brown Pelican and Reddish Egret populations on the Central Texas coast, and interior Least Tern and Cattle Egret populations elsewhere. And, with census figures gathered during the yearly Texas Colonial Waterbird Census, the TPWD monitors populations and population changes from year to year.

The U.S. Fish and Wildlife Service (USFWS) is also increasing its efforts to protect the colonial wading birds, by participating in the Texas Colonial Waterbird Census, monitoring populations and population changes, and working in conjunction with the Corps of Engineers to use the dredged material from the maintenance of the Intracoastal Waterway and other ship channels to build new nesting islands or rebuild islands that have suffered erosion.

During the late 1800's and early 1900's, the Roseate Spoonbills, and several of the egrets, terns, and gulls were driven almost to extinction by plume hunters and egg gatherers. After laws were passed banning these practices, the birds were able to reestablish their populations because large wilderness areas existed. Today in the continental United States only token wilderness areas exist. None are large enough to be self-sustaining; all require human intervention. National Audubon wardens patrol their islands, but on other islands, the birds have to fend for themselves and are often disturbed by anglers, campers, and sightseers. Increasing population pressure and new problems, such as fire ants, require that this group of birds receive active attention from government agencies and also the care and concern of every person who uses and enjoys the out-of-doors.

I do not intend this book to be a bird identification guide; there are already several very good ones in print. It is, rather, a diary of close observations of nesting habits and the little dramas that occur in the birds' lives, an accounting of the historical problems the birds had, and a sketch of the present ecological problems the birds are facing.

Acknowledgments

A project of this nature is never a one-person undertaking. I started this project in total ignorance of what it might take to complete it. Had it not been for some very special people who offered encouragement and suggestions, patiently answered my questions, and did preliminary proofreading, this book would never have been completed. I want to give special thanks to:

Elric McHenry who introduced me to the colonial wading birds.

Suzanne Bloom, Professor of Art, University of Houston, for her encouragement and a crash course in writing.

Alan Mueller, U.S. Fish and Wildlife Service, for his suggestions and a superb job of proofreading.

I also want to thank John Tveten for his constant encouragement and Ted Eubanks for always being available to answer questions. Jesse Grantham, formerly of the National Audubon Society, arranged for my visits to the NAS sanctuaries in Laguna Madre and Ray Little, NAS warden, provided the best guide service one could imagine. Roy and Karen Christoffel supplied some valuable historical information. And the staff at the University of Texas Press have been a real pleasure to work with.

Group Names

An important part of being a hunter in the medieval days was knowing the language of the hunt, part of which was knowing the proper names of the animal groups. The earliest surviving list is from the *Edgerton Manuscript* from about A.D. 1450. *The Book of St. Albans,* which appeared in 1486, had the most complete list of animal and social terms. The book lists ninety-four animal terms and seventy social terms which pertained to people and life in the fifteenth century, including "a congregation of people," "a converting of preachers," and "a sentence of judges." The lists from *The Book of St. Albans* and many new terms are found in *An Exaltation of Larks* by James Lipton.

Nye of pheasants
Bouquet of pheasants
Badling of ducks
Paddling of ducks

Gaggle of geese (on water)
Skein of geese (flying)
Fall of woodcock

Wisp of snipe
Walk of snipe
Exaltation of larks
Murmuration of starlings

Brood of hens
Covey of partridges
Murder of crows
Rafter of turkeys
Dule of doves

Dissimulation of birds
Peep of chickens
Pitying of turtledoves
Siege of herons

Charm of finches
Cast of hawks
Deceit of lapwings

Building of rooks
Ostentation of peacocks
Tidings of magpies
Congregation of plovers
Unkindness of ravens

Host of sparrows
Descent of woodpeckers
Mustering of storks
Clutch of eggs
Flight of swallows

Watch of nightingales
Parliament of owls
Gulp of cormorants (James Lipton)
Stand of flamingoes (James Lipton)

To this list I add
a "splattering of gulls"
and a "cacophony of terns"

American White Pelicans are very social birds, enjoying each other's company whether they are feeding, nesting, or just resting.

The brilliant blue on the lores of the Reddish Egret and the bright green on the lores of the Great Egrets will fade early in the nesting season.

Each pair of Royal Terns, on Little Pelican Island, lays one turkey-sized egg in a shallow scrape in the open sand flats or shell banks.

A White Ibis prepares for takeoff after bathing in a shallow pool.

A Tricolored Heron stands guard over its nest at Rollover Pass.

Least Terns can find a
home and thrive in the
hostile environment of
Redfish Island if their
nesting sites are not
overrun by people and
their pets.

Was this someone's
joke or did the Roseate
Spoonbill find this
fishing cork and place
it in its nest?

White-faced Ibis.

A Cattle Egret shows off its full breeding plumage.

*This Sandwich and Royal Tern colony is on the western bank of
Little Pelican Island.*

An Olivaceous Cormorant must dry its wings periodically after feeding underwater.

This young Forster's Tern looks exactly like a Laughing Gull chick but, at the same age, is slightly smaller.

A prickly pear cactus thicket provides protection from predators for four Reddish Egret nests.

The parent Caspian Tern is having a discussion with its chick.

Youngsters demand food as soon as their parent returns to the nest.

Nesting Birds of the Coastal Islands

First it rained, and then it snew
Then it friz, and then it thew
and then it friz again
(ANON.)

The Islands

My islands sleep through January. They need long, deep rests after very busy years. Not only are they subjected to constant pressure from the wind and water, but every year for countless centuries, the Galveston Bay area has been host to some fifty thousand pairs of nesting colonial wading birds, gulls, and terns. All of Texas' colonial birds except the pelicans nest here: the herons, egrets, gulls, terns, spoonbills, ibises, and cormorants. Brown Pelicans were observed nesting at San Luis Pass at the west end of Galveston Bay in the 1930's, but there have been none since.

From the birds' standpoint the islands are ideal, providing the isolation and security they must have for the intense nesting period. The islands offer no direct sustenance, but this is readily found in the shallow bay waters and marshes within easy flying distance. In size the islands are large enough to offer some permanence, but only three, Pelican, Little Pelican, and North Deer islands, are large enough to harbor predator populations, that is, rats, Western diamondback rattlesnakes, and king snakes. Of the three, only Pelican Island can provide a reliable supply of fresh water that larger predators, such as raccoons and opossums, need. From year to year the birds succeed because of their sheer numbers and the isolation of the

Opposite page:
This shell bank on Little Pelican Island, which looks so desolate in January, will be a prime nesting place for Black Skimmers, Laughing Gulls, and Royal and Sandwich Terns in April and May.

islands, in spite of the fact that they are surrounded by one of the largest metropolitan populations in the United States.

The islands' unusual variety of habitats makes it possible for all the colonial birds to find suitable nesting sites. No one island offers all the preferred habitats, but somewhere in the bay each of the species can find an island with the shell banks, acres of sand flats, marsh grasses, large bushes, or trees that it requires. There are, in Galveston County alone, more than thirty nesting areas. Of these I selected eight on which to photograph because of their accessibility and the variety of species found on each one.

North Deer Island, a National Audubon Society (NAS) sanctuary, is a natural island that was enlarged during the construction of the Intracoastal Waterway. The birds gather on North Deer earlier than on the other islands nearby, but with large areas of deep brush, prickly pear cactus, and large rattlesnakes, it is a difficult and dangerous place for photography.

South Deer Island, a low, marshy, natural island, usually hosts one of the two Caspian Tern colonies in the immediate vicinity. Black Skimmers, Laughing Gulls, and Forster's Terns find that the island's narrow banks make excellent nesting places. A band of high ground across the center of the island supports scrubby trees and bushes in which Tricolored Herons, Snowy Egrets, and White-faced Ibises find secure nesting.

The Down Deer Islands are small islands east of North Deer Island. Caspian Terns, Laughing Gulls, and usually a pair of American Oystercatchers nest here. These islands are declining in importance since they are eroding away.

The Swan Lake rookery hosts Black Skimmers, Forster's Terns, and Gull-billed Terns. The Swan Lake area was once a narrow, mile-long shell bank with nesting places for herons and egrets. It is also a declining rookery because the shell bank has suffered severe erosion problems.

Little Pelican Island, one of the most important nesting islands on the Texas coast, is not an NAS sanctuary, but definitely needs to be. It is a natural island that has been built up with dredged material. A long, wide shell bank and open sand flats make excellent nesting sites for Royal and Sandwich terns, Laughing Gulls, and Black Skimmers, while low, dense bushy areas give sanctuary to Black-crowned Night-Herons, Tricolored Herons, Snowy Egrets, and White Ibises. Newly arrived, ever-expanding salt cedar growths on the high ground on the east and central part of the island are inhabited by all the herons and egrets, Roseate Spoonbills, and Olivaceous Cormorants.

In Moses Lake and Dickinson Bay are a series of small spoil islands on which Black Skimmers, Forster's Terns, and a few Laughing Gulls nest. These islands are not always used; some years the birds nest on them, other years they don't.

Redfish Island is a narrow, mile-long shell bank paralleling the Houston Ship Channel in the central part of Galveston Bay that, like Swan Lake, is eroding away. Least Terns, Black Skimmers, and Forster's Terns regularly nest there, but have difficulty because of the number of people that use the island for camping, picnicking, and fishing. Some even bring their dogs onshore.

The Rollover Pass Islands are the latest additions to the list of NAS sanctuaries. They are also my favorite islands for photographing the herons, spoonbills, and cormorants. These small spoil islands have marshes, sand flats, and open grassy areas with interspersed bushes that seldom grow more than 3 feet tall. The large birds nest in the low bushes and on the ground, making it relatively easy to photograph into their nests.

During the mild coastal winters the islands provide secure roosting for Brown and American White pelicans, Laughing, Ring-billed, and Herring gulls, Royal Terns, Great Egrets, and Great Blue Herons. The salt and brackish waters of the Texas coast supply winter feeding grounds for Double-crested Cormorants, Common Loons, and many varieties of ducks.

The egrets' breeding plumage and the Laughing Gulls' black heads indicate that, in January, the nesting season is about to begin. The early nesters will start gathering in February, and the late nesters do not leave until September. They dig holes in the sand and shell banks, trample the short grasses, fill the trees, bushes, and grassy areas with their nests, and whitewash the trees with their droppings. In turn, the insects and bacteria that live in the soil work twenty-four hours a day to turn the tons of each year's guano into fertilizer to feed the vegetation.

February the short, is woorst of al.
(JOHN FLORIO, "FIRSTE FRUITES," 1578)

The Gathering

FEBRUARY

February is the month of the gathering of the birds. The Great Blue Herons, Great Egrets, and all the other herons, egrets, and cormorants are "loners" most of the year; that is, they tend to feed alone, but when breeding time comes, gather in great or small colonies (hence the term "colonial") on isolated islands or other safe places. White Ibises, social birds, always feeding and traveling in flocks, join the colonies to select areas where they can nest as a group or mix their nests with those of the herons and egrets.

Large numbers of birds arrive on North Deer Island earlier in the season than the other islands in the Galveston Bay complex, early arrivals getting the best nesting sites. I photographed and observed on North Deer at the start of the season, then moved to the other islands as the birds arrived on them. Great Blue Herons, in their breeding plumage, start arriving in early February to mate, select sites, and build nests in the prime spots of the best trees and bushes. Their nests are large and require many sticks, more than are available on the island, so they have to make 4- to 5-mile round trips to the mainland for building materials. Often, in the evenings I anchor my boat off the west shoreline and watch them come across the bay, sometimes not 3 feet off the water, each carrying a single stick in its beak.

Opposite page:
Private boat and barge traffic is continuous in the Intracoastal Waterway. As long as the tugboats don't sound their horns the birds on the spoil island rookeries don't pay any attention to them.

North Deer Island, an NAS sanctuary, is well established as one of the most important nesting islands on the Texas Gulf Coast. It is a natural island that was enlarged during the building of the Intracoastal Waterway, and now covers 160 acres. Along the western side nearest the waterway the builders piled great mounds of clay that I sometimes refer to as the "ridges." These are now covered with brush, trees, and cacti that provide excellent nesting sites for the herons, egrets, spoonbills, cormorants, and White Ibis. The eastern side of the island, still in its natural state, is made up of sand flats and marsh and is a favorite nesting place for Laughing Gulls, White-faced Ibis, and Forster's Terns.

Reddish Egret

Egretta rufescens
FAMILY: ARDEIDAE

Egret is derived from the Old High German *heiger,* "heron," by adding the diminutive *-ette* to give *hegr-ette.* In Old French *egrette* meant "fowl, like a heron." *Egretta* is the Latinized form of *egret.* In the revised *Birds of North America and Canada,* Nuttall (1919) lists the Reddish Egret as *Ardea rufescens;* in the *Life Histories of North American Marsh Birds,* U.S. National Museum Bulletin No. 135, Bent (1926) lists it as *Dichromanassa rufescens.* In 1983 the Committee on Classification and Nomenclature of the American Ornithologists Union changed it, and one hopes for the last time, to *Egretta rufescens.* Of all the names, *Dichromanassa* is by far the most interesting, being a combination of the Greek *dis,* "twice," *chroma,* "color," and *anassa,* "queen," to give "two-colored queen." *Rufescens* is Latin for "reddish" or "turning red" and describes the bird's color. Other common names include the muffle-jawed egret, Peale's egret (white phase), and plume bird.

In the United States the Reddish Egret breeds locally on the Texas and Louisiana Gulf Coast and from Tampa, Florida, south to the Keys. It also breeds on both coasts of Mexico and in the Bahamas, West Indies, and Central America. Some individuals remain on the Gulf Coast during the winter months, but most move south along coastal Mexico to El Salvador. Nonetheless, the Reddish Egret has the most limited geographical and ecological range of any of the herons and, since it is strictly coastal, seldom ranges inland to fresh-water feeding grounds. Reddish Egrets prefer to nest in low trees and bushes, where they build flat stick platforms with no lining of any sort. They will also nest on the ground, fashioning deep-cavitied nests from the surrounding grasses.

Because of its dichromatism the Reddish Egret caused much confusion and controversy among the early naturalists and scientists. At first the white phase appeared as a distinct species with the name "Peale's egret." John James Audubon thought the white Peale's egret was the normal plumage of the immature Reddish Egret. By the 1920's the dispute seems to have been settled with the white bird being accepted as a regular, but unusual, color phase. There is also the "pied" form which shows both white and reddish feathers. Both the white- and red-phase birds show the distinctive pink, black-tipped bills and the cobalt blue legs. In the breeding season

Opposite page:
White and red-phase Reddish Egrets, seen here together, nest and breed together with no discrimination whatsoever.

the plumes on the neck and head give the Reddish Egrets a shaggy look.

In the latter part of the nineteenth and early part of the twentieth centuries the Reddish Egrets, along with the Great and Snowy egrets, fell in enormous numbers to the guns of the plume hunters. In 1926, the ornithologist A. C. Bent remarked, "It was the same story with many other localities; and today I doubt if the Reddish Egret breeds anywhere in Florida." To study the Reddish Egret, Bent visited the middle and lower Texas coastline, which provided a good habitat in long bays and on low marshy islands. The plume hunters were after the nuptial plumes, which they acquired by shooting the adult breeding birds off the nests. In the *Life Histories of North American Marsh Birds,* Bent quotes W. E. D. Scott (1887), who wrote of the destruction on the Florida coast. Mr. Scott described in graphic detail the destruction the plume hunters wrought as they shot the adult birds, took the breeding feathers and some wings, and left the eggs, young birds, and adult carcasses to be devoured by fish crows and buzzards.

No doubt the plume hunters found the birds easy prey. The Reddish Egrets are the extroverts in the bird colony, sitting on a high branch showing off their plumage, constantly turning to watch other birds in the colony, flaring their plumage to all passers-by. The plumes, bristled out, give the bird a conspicuous, bizarre appearance and resemble quills or spiked hairdos more than feathers. Even more of a threat to the bird is the fact that in the nesting stage they are very easy to approach. Several times I have stood in plain view and photographed displaying Reddish Egrets without their taking flight.

Reddish Egrets and Black-crowned Night-Herons also gather in February. Reddish Egrets, establishing their territories, perch on the tops of the bushes, to peck at all passers-by in defense of their nesting sites and, in doing so, display their spectacular plumage. Like the White Ibises, a hundred or more of the Reddish Egrets may establish nests in an area all

to themselves or mix their nests randomly with those of the other colonial birds. They and the Black-crowned Night-Herons select nesting sites in the brush and prickly pear thickets on the slopes of the ridges. Roseate Spoonbills gather to feed in the little inlets around the marsh, but seem to prefer warmer weather for nesting. Little Blue Herons usually nest near freshwater sites but there are always five to ten pairs breeding on North Deer Island.

This blind, having full standing headroom, is my favorite for photographing down into nests. Its drawback is that it must be staked down.

In the brush and on the ponds and bays around the island, the winter birds, such as Pipits, Horned Larks, warblers, Ruddy Ducks, Northern Pintails, American Coots, Blue and Green-winged teals, and grebes, mix with the summer birds, such as Black-necked Stilts, Seaside Sparrows, and the ever-present Great-tailed Grackles. February is a wonderful time to be out birding.

My indoor project for the month of February was to design and build a permanent blind to be set up on Little Pelican Island in an egret nesting area. The floor measured 4 feet square and the walls were 5 feet high. It was built in my garage so that it could be disassembled, carried to the island, and quickly reassembled in place. The blind was 5 feet off the ground on pipe legs with "T's" as horizontal extensions on the bottoms of the legs to anchor the structure into the ground. When a decent day came, I loaded the blind, nuts and bolts, shovel, and toolbox into the boat and headed for the island.

After scouting Little Pelican Island, I selected a clear spot on the north side that had good access and was ringed by 5-foot-tall bushes. In years before, Great Egrets, Great Blue Herons, Tricolored Herons, Black-crowned Night-Herons, and Cattle Egrets had nested here. I anchored the boat as close as possible and carried parts ashore through deep, dense brush, beating down a semblance of a path after several trips. The area where the blind was to be set is sand, so digging the 2-foot holes for the legs was no problem. I assembled the legs and floor, set the legs into their holes, leveled the floor somewhat, and refilled the holes. Next I attached a short ladder and bolted the sides and top on. Somehow this "easy" project turned into a full day of solid work.

Once the blind was up I could look through the portholes into the tops of all the nearby bushes. I wouldn't know for about two months whether I had picked a good spot for photographing or whether I had just wasted a lot of time and energy.

Late in February, on one of those incredible, blue-sky, 80-degree days, I went back to watch the birds on North Deer Island. The island was a beautiful lush green, the grasses were coming up, and the bushes and trees, all leafed out and growing vigorously, were putting last year's guano to good use. Early nesters were arriving in full force. The birds, in the process of selecting sites for and building their nests, were difficult to approach for photographing, so for most of the time I kept my distance and watched through binoculars.

Olivaceous Cormorants were among the early arrivals. Some chose to mix their nests with those of Great Blue Herons and Roseate Spoonbills in the 25-foot-tall trees on the northeast ridge and in the north central part of the island.

A group of about fifty spoonbills, feeding in a shallow cove, took flight as soon as I stepped foot on shore even though I was 200–300 yards away. Another hundred were scattering their nests in among the herons and egrets.

About two hundred Reddish Egrets established their territories on the slope of the southwest-most ridge in the scrubby bushes and prickly pear cactus. White-phase Reddish Egrets are uncommon, but they mate and nest indiscriminately with red-phase birds. Most of their nests were built, but there were no signs of eggs. I set up my portable blind near the colony and photographed one "pied" bird with white secondary wing feathers. Some close-up photographs of the Reddish Egrets showed the most beautiful blue patch at the base of their bill and around their eye, which faded as the nesting season progressed.

A skittish Yellow-crowned Night-Heron was nesting with the Reddish Egrets, which was unusual because they prefer nesting alone or in small, inland colonies. Most years none are reported; one year ten were seen.

Twenty or thirty Great Egrets and a half-dozen Black-crowned Night-Herons were selecting nesting sites near the Reddish Egrets. A dozen White Ibises were feeding along the tidal margin, but not nesting yet. Later, there may be more than a thousand.

I was walking along the shell bank enjoying the bird sounds, the fresh air, and the warm sun, when I spotted a solitary American Oystercatcher nest with three eggs. The parents, feeding on an exposed oyster reef just off shore, were taking a big chance because the weather could still turn very foul.

Like the moneth of March,
which entreth like a Lion,
but goeth out like a lamb.
(JAMES HOWELL, "DONDA'S GROVE," 1640)

When March comes in with an adder's head,
   it goes out with a peacock's tail:
when March comes in with a peacock's tail,
   it goes out with an adder's head.
(SCOTTISH SAYING)

Nest Building and Breeding

MARCH

The egret and heron nesting areas on all the islands really come alive in March. This is the month when these large birds gather into their colonies in increasing numbers, to mate, build nests, and lay eggs. The ones that arrived in February will be incubating eggs, and by the latter part of March, will have small chicks. Laughing Gulls will be gathering but not nesting yet, and the terns won't show up for another month.

By early March, about 150 Great Blue Herons had built nests in the trees along the ridges on North Deer Island. Two hundred Roseate Spoonbills, 150 Olivaceous Cormorants, and 250 Great Egrets mixed their nests in with those of the great blues. Some 250 Reddish Egrets took over a hillside at the south end of the ridges. When I anchored the boat just off the Intracoastal Waterway on the west side of the island and surveyed the ridges and nesting areas through binoculars, there seemed to be a vertical pecking order. In general, the Great Blue Herons had the highest spots, the Great Egrets and cormorants the next highest, while all the other small herons and egrets found nesting sites in the low bushes. I walked into the trees and found that one of the Great Egrets' nests contained an egg,

Opposite page:
Eggs must be turned
every few hours so that
the yolk doesn't sink to
the bottom and stick
to the shell.

and moved quickly away so the birds could return to tend their nests. Some Great Blue Herons had already finished their nests and were incubating eggs. Last year's nests, in a state of disrepair, were being reworked, which is logical because they were already in the best sites—in solid forks of the trees and bushes. One tree had four Great Blue Heron or Great Egret nests. A scrubby tree contained four small nests; another, five. The smaller nests would be occupied by Snowy Egrets or Tricolored Herons, but there were no signs of eggs. A thousand or so Laughing Gulls, not quite ready to build nests, gathered on the shell banks. One Ring-billed Gull, soon to be heading north, was loitering with the Laughing Gulls.

Great Blue Heron

Ardea herodias
FAMILY: ARDEIDAE

The king of the colony, the Great Blue Heron, rests while the wind blows its feathers.

The word *heron* has an ancient and varied background. It came into the Middle English from Old French and has similar derivations in the Scandinavian languages. Old High German *heiger* or *heigir* came into Old Frensh as *hairon* and into Old Provençal as *aigros,* which yields the Italian *aghirone* or *airone* and the Spanish *airon*. The Scandinavian forms are *hager* (Swedish) and *heire* (Danish), each meaning "heron." Old English *hragra,* "heron," may be related to German *reiher* and Dutch *reiger,* which are allied to Greek *kriein,* "to cry out or shriek."

Herodias is Greek for "heron." *Ardea* is Latin for "heron." At various times and places the Great Blue Heron has been called big cranky, blue crane, crane, gray crane, long John, poor Joe, and red-shouldered heron.

The Great Blue Heron is the largest and most stately of the colonial birds, standing about 4 feet tall. The large size and the overall blue-gray color set this bird apart from any other in the United States. It is the most widely dispersed heron in North America, breeding on the Alaskan Peninsula, across southern Canada to Nova Scotia, south through the United States, Mexico, West Indies and the Galapagos Islands.

Oberholser (*The Bird Life of Texas*) listed three subspecies of the Great Blue Heron in Texas.

- Eastern Great Blue Heron, *Ardea herodias herodias* Linnaeus. Breeding range: Eastern United States and Southern Canada.
- Ward's Great Blue Heron, *Ardea herodias wardi* Ridge-way. Breeding range: Central and southeastern United States.
- Treganza's Great Blue Heron, *Ardea herodias treganzai* Court. Breeding range: Western United States except the Pacific Coast area.

The Great White Heron of southern Florida (and occasionally Texas) is now considered to be a color phase of the Great Blue Heron. Both Bent and Oberholser listed the Great White Heron, *Ardea occidentalis,* as a separate species. Bent was very positive about their being separate, while Oberholser held open the possibility of their being color phases of the same species.

On the ridges of North Deer Island the birds have a definite pecking order. Great Blue Herons, being the largest, and among the earliest nesters, take the choice places in the tree tops, tall bushes, or clumps of prickly pear cactus. In other parts of the country they will nest on rock ledges, sea cliffs, on the ground, or in the tops of large trees. Nesting materials will be whatever is available. Great Blue Heron nests are large, 25 to 40 inches in diameter, moderately cupped, and, because they are so large, need the support of a substantial bush or tree. Young Great Blue Herons don't move around the colony like some of their neighbors but stay on the nest until they are grown and fully fledged.

The mean temperature on the Gulf Coast in late spring and summer is extremely hot, and the heron's nests, being in the tops of the trees and bushes, are exposed to the full summer sun. Young herons, egrets, and cormorants cool themselves the same way dogs do—by panting. They sit on the nest in the full summer sun, mouths open, moving air rapidly in and out of their lungs, cooling themselves by evaporation.

In the salt cedar grove on the northeast corner of Little Pelican Island, twenty Great Blue Herons and some Great Egrets were establishing nests. Out on the sand flats, more than a thousand Laughing Gulls were roosting, but staying close overhead when I walked through. As I intruded into their territory, they took off, hovered overhead, and settled back down as I passed. There were no nests, but they were feeling the beginnings of the mating urges.

The Rollover Pass Islands are the latest additions to the list of NAS sanctuaries on the Texas coast, having come under their jurisdiction in 1988. Originally there were eleven of these spoil islands in East Galveston Bay. Seven have eroded away, leaving four, with a total area of about 3 acres.

More than 250 American White Pelicans were on a nearby shell bank getting ready for the trip to their northern breeding grounds in the Prairie Provinces of Canada and the north central part of the United States. Seventy-five Great Egrets, forty Olivaceous Cormorants and three pairs of Great Blue Herons were establishing territories on the largest of the Rollover Pass Islands. Although there were no finished nests or eggs, platform construction had been started and their claims were already getting the whitewashed look. At this time of year the birds are very wary; their so-called "critical range," or the distance that they will allow humans to approach, is very long. They moved off 200–300 yards and watched me intently when I arrived. This "critical range" shortens significantly when there are eggs or nestlings. I stayed on the island for about fifteen minutes, just long enough for a quick survey, got back in the boat, drifted away from the island, and watched the egrets take off and circle back over the nesting area. One by one they circled around, made their final approach upwind, and settled gently back on their nest. When well away from the island, I started my engine and headed home. Riding back to the launching ramp, I saw a lone Brown Pelican feeding along the Intracoastal Waterway. Brown Pelicans are making a comeback now that the miracle chemicals DDT and dieldrin, which got into their food chain and affected their eggshell-making ability, have been banned. It was good to see them again after a twenty-year absence.

Olivaceous Cormorant

Phalacrocorax olivaceus
FAMILY: PHALACROCORACIDAE

An Olivaceous Cormorant family, three young birds on the left, the parent on the right, is about to leave the colony for the year.

The Olivaceous Cormorant has undergone several name changes. Bent listed it as *Phalacrocorax vigua mexicanus,* in Oberholser it was *P. brasilianus,* and it is now *P. olivaceus.*

Let's hope it is less confused by all the name changing than we are. The word *cormorant* comes from the Romance languages and means "sea crow." It came into English from the Old French *cormaran,* which was derived from *corp,* "crow," and *marenc,* "belonging to the sea." In Middle French the word changed to *comerant.* In the Celtic languages, Breton and Welsh, the word is *morvran* and *morfran,* from *mor,* "the sea," and *bran,* "crow."

Phalacrocoracidae is from the Greek *phalakrokorax,* from *phalakros,* "bald," and *korax,* "raven." Pliny (A.D. 23–79) used the word, but we don't know what he was referring to. Cormorants do not look bald. *Olivaceus* is from the Latin for "olive color." Close up, the birds have a beautiful metallic olive sheen, but it is not a useful field mark. They look black from a distance.

The Olivaceous Cormorant is the smallest of the three cormorants living on the Gulf and Atlantic coasts. The original name was Mexican Cormorant, but it has also been called the Neotropic, Bigua, and Brazilian cormorant by various authors. Its breeding range extends from south Louisiana and Texas to Nicaragua, Cuba, the Bahamas, south to the Amazon, and west to high Andean lakes. Some species members winter along the Texas and Louisiana coasts, but most move south where the water is warmer.

At Rollover Pass some were nesting in very low bushes near the edge of the water. On North Deer Island others beat out some Great Blue Herons for a few spots in the highest trees. The cormorants build stick nests 15–20 inches across and 4–6 inches deep. Each pair lays two to five chalky white eggs that are about the size of chicken eggs, but more elongated. The young, when hatched, are textbook examples of the term *altricial,* from the Latin *altrix,* meaning "nurse" or "wet nurse," for chicks that hatch in a completely helpless condition. The young cormorants are totally naked, have their eyes closed, are unable to leave the nest, and are totally dependent on their parents. In *The Audubon Society Encyclopedia of North American Birds,* John Terres tells us that eggs containing the altricial young have a smaller relative yolk size, 15–25 percent of the egg weight, than those of the precocial young, 25–50 percent of the egg weight. Thus the precocial young are fed better in the egg and are much stronger and more developed after hatching. The parents of altricial young, like our cormorants, usually build substantial nests in trees where the young are safe from predators.

On a beautiful day in the middle of March I went back to the largest of the Rollover Pass Islands and set up my blind on the west side of the knoll where the larger birds nest. Olivaceous Cormorants are the earliest nesters; some were already incubating eggs. In the first two hours I saw six pairs of Great Egrets and two pairs of Great Blue Herons mating, and of these I managed to photograph two of the Great Egrets and one of the Great Blue Herons. A group of twenty-five Roseate Spoonbills and fifteen White Ibises landed in an open grassy area 40 yards away. Two of the spoonbills seemed to be building a nest on a low bush, while others were lowering their heads and chasing one another, just for short distances, not aggressively. This could be a mating performance, or they could be chasing a rival away.

A Great Egret was systematically dismantling a neighboring cormorant's nest. From where I was sitting, the Great Egret's nest appeared to be below and behind the cormorant's. Time after time the egret stepped up on its neighbor's nest, pulled a stick out, and returned to its nest. Sometimes it would grasp a live branch of a bush, pull as hard as it could, using its wings for added power, finally realize something was wrong, and look for easier pickings. The cormorant returned to find its nest in disorder and proceeded to repair its own by borrowing sticks from another neighbor's nest.

Two Great Egrets worked the whole day trying to attract mates, standing with their backs to the wind so that their breeding feathers were blown out around them like halos. Repeatedly they bent their knees, dipped their heads, stretched their necks, and pointed their beaks to the sky. Watching them was simply spellbinding. By the end of the day I had seen ten pairs of egrets mating.

Great Egret

Casmerodius albus
FAMILY: ARDEIDAE

Attracting a mate is serious business. This Great Egret did his "mating dance" all day without any success, at least while I was watching.

The current genus name *Casmerodius* is made up from the Greek *chasma*, "open mouth," and *herodias*, "heron," thus meaning "open-mouthed heron." This bird is definitely not open-mouthed. The name may have been given for the gap, or commissure, between the upper and lower mandibles that in this species, unlike other herons, extends well behind the eye. Another explanation, more esthetically appealing, is that the name may be due to a misspelling of *cosmerodius,* from the Greek *kosmos,* or "decoration." In its breeding plumage, the great egret is certainly a decorated heron. *Albus,* in Latin means "white." The older ornithologists listed the Great Egret by several different names: in the A. C. Bent series it is listed as the American Egret, *C. egretta;* in Nuttall as *Ardea egretta;* and in Oberholser as the Common Egret, *C. albus.* No bird as elegant as this should be called "common." To the plume hunters of Florida it was known as long white. Other common names have been angel bird, big plume bird, great white egret, plume bird, and white crane.

To call this bird an American egret is a misnomer since it is found on all the continents except Antarctica. It is at home in both salt and fresh water. The United States breeding range extends from Oregon to California, along the Gulf Coast from Texas to Florida, through the Midwest to the Great Lakes, and along the Atlantic Coast as far north as Maine. The slightly smaller size, heavy yellow bill, and black legs differentiate it from the Great White Heron of southern Florida.

The killing of the egrets, terns, and other birds for the millinery trade, which started during Audubon's time (1840) and continued into the early twentieth century, was one of the low points in the history of people's relationship with other animals. All that destruction for greed's and vanity's sake—just so women could wear pretty feathers and whole birds on their hats. The plume hunters carried their guns to the East and Gulf coasts of the United States, South and Central America, Australia, and anyplace else the birds lived. As is true of so much of the destruction of the natural world, the driving force behind the killing was profit. In Bent's *Life Histories of North American Marsh Birds* (1926), Herbert K. Job (1905) stated that in 1903 the price for plumes offered to hunters was $32 per ounce, which made the plumes worth about twice their weight in gold. He went on to write that at the London Commercial Sales Rooms during 1902, 1,608 thirty-ounce packages of "ospreys," that is, herons' plumes, were sold, for a total of 48,240 ounces. About four birds are required to yield an ounce of plumes, which meant that 192,960 herons were killed at their nests, and that two to three times that number of young or eggs were destroyed.

The plumes are at their prime early in the nesting season. As the season progresses the plumes get bent and broken and are eventually shed; so to get fresh, clean feathers, the hunters shot the birds off their nests, leaving the eggs to rot or the chicks to starve. No thought was ever given to the future as whole rookeries were annihilated. The people in the millinery trade circulated the story that the feathers were picked up from the ground in the rookeries after being shed by the birds, which was the story many people wanted to believe. In all the time I have been photographing these birds I have found only a half-dozen plumes. A few "dead plumes" were picked up and sold, but they brought only one-fifth the price of "live plumes." A. C. Bent, in his Life Histories Series, published an interview with T. Gilbert Pearson (1912), an old plume hunter, in which he described the horrors of plume hunting in Venezuela and Colombia. Pearson said that the plume dealer's claim of only selling shed plumes was a lie and went on to describe in graphic terms the brutality against these magnificent birds.

The Great Egret populations were reduced less than those of the Snowy Egret, but as late as 1923 only three breeding colonies were found on the Texas Coast. The Great Egret is somewhat shyer and its long stiff feathers were less desirable in the millinery trade than those of the Snowy Egret. After World War I the demand for the feathers decreased and the population rebounded, reaching its historic numbers in the 1920's and 1930's. The Great Egrets' eggs were affected by DDT, but not as severely as those of Brown Pelicans and some others. Since the 1972 ban on the chemical, clutch and brood sizes have increased to pre-DDT levels. Their nesting sites are reasonably secure on the coastal islands, but even as Oberholser noted years ago, "Most mainland colonies have been developed out of existence."

On North Deer Island in the latter part of March, one Great Blue Heron nest on the north end of the ridges had three eggs; two more had two each. Another had three very young chicks. Some of the Great Egret nests had one or two eggs; others were empty. Reddish Egrets found safety from predators on a second ridge, which was covered with prickly pear cactus. I didn't see any nests but there may have been some down in the cactus. Rattlesnakes love this terrain, so I am always careful. Eight hundred or so White Ibises were nesting in a canebrake just over the hill from the Reddish Egrets. They had broken down most of the cane, and the nests were on or near the ground, but there were no eggs. Another group of about five hundred was gathering nearby in some dense growths of prickly pear cactus, but they hadn't built their nests yet. Some years, as few as three hundred White Ibises nest on the island.

Little Pelican Island, a natural island of about 120 acres, was once part of Pelican Island until it was cut off by the building of the Intracoastal Waterway. Around 1980, spoil from the dredging of the waterway was pumped across the central part of the island, raising the level of the island and smothering all the vegetation. After that, salt cedar established itself, grew profusely, and now provides nesting for all the larger birds. White Ibises and the smaller herons and egrets find excellent nesting in acres of almost impenetrable brush. Laughing Gulls nest on sand flats on the north and south sides of the island and along the three-quarter-mile-long shell bank bordering the west side. Royal and Sandwich terns and Black Skimmers dig their nests along this same shell bank, while White-faced Ibises find security in a salt marsh on the south side of the island.

On Little Pelican Island a flock of Laughing Gulls was scattered along the shell bank just north of where I always anchor my boat. More were gathered on the sand flats on the north, east, and south sides of the island but none were nesting. An American Oystercatcher nest with one egg was out on the open shell bank, well away from the other birds. About seventy-five Sandwich Terns were gathered into a small colony on the western shell bank near the northwest corner of the island. They moved on down the bank as I approached but

The male Great Egret approaches the female, mates with her in a brief but frantic ritual, and retires to a nearby bush.

were, apparently, establishing nests. There were no scrapes or eggs. Farther on was a fresh dead Double-crested Cormorant that had caught its neck in one hole of a plastic six-pack holder and starved to death. Another victim of trashy people.

The salt cedar, taking over on the northeast end of the island, grows fast, is very bushy, and seems to provide good nesting. There were two to six nests in each tree. Great Blue Herons, Reddish Egrets, Great Egrets, and Olivaceous Cormorants were on their nests incubating eggs. A Roseate Spoonbill flew over carrying a stick for its nest. I discovered one clump of salt cedar containing the remains of fourteen nests. Later, these were claimed and rebuilt by the Snowy and Reddish egrets, Tricolored Herons, Black-crowned Night-Herons, and some White Ibises. More than one hundred Black-crowned Night-Herons were secreting nests down inside the low, dense scrub. I stay out of this area during nesting season. The scrub is hip-to-chest deep and so dense that the nests could be upset and destroyed before anyone would be aware of their presence.

My surveying complete, I went back to the boat, drifted away from the island, started the engine, and headed back to the dock. Suddenly, my propeller hit something solid, jarring the whole boat. I instinctively pulled the throttle back, looked over my shoulder, and saw something flapping on the surface of the water. I circled around and came upwind to see what this flapping thing was. Apparently I had hit a fisherman's gill net and entangled a Common Loon in its weave. It took a great effort to untwist and cut, and finally free the loon, whose knee joint on the right leg was broken. For a loon this is very bad. Because their legs are so far back on their bodies they can't really walk on land; they just push themselves along on their chests, and without the knee joint they can't swim. The break was fresh and was probably caused when the boat hit the net. I put the loon on the floor of the boat and hurried to the dock. Though it was late when I arrived, I was able to contact the wildlife rehabilitation people who, when they saw the bird, were disheartened. The prognosis for a loon with a severely broken leg is very poor. Anyone who sets a gill net to snare all species of fish—marketable or not—also kills, however inadvertently, these beautiful birds.

Holsom as the Aprile showr fallyng on the herbes newe.
(JOHN LYNGATE, "REASON AND SENSUALITY,"
L. 6310, C. 1430)

Nests and Eggs

APRIL

April is the month for laying and incubating eggs and caring for newly hatched chicks. April is also the month that we start to see the overlap in the birds' nesting seasons. While the majority of the herons, egrets, and cormorants will be incubating eggs or caring for chicks, others will just be establishing nests, and the Laughing Gulls, terns, and White-faced Ibises will be starting nests. The earliest of the Black Skimmers will be laying eggs in their small scrapes on the shell banks, while others will wait until summer, sometimes as late as August, to nest. The long nesting seasons on the Gulf Coast contrast sharply with the brief but frantic nesting seasons in the far north, where summers are short.

By the first of April, all of the nests of the Great and Snowy egrets, Roseate Spoonbills, and Olivaceous Cormorants at Rollover Pass had eggs. The Great Egret chicks were hatching, and judging from their size, some were at least a week old. Others were just hours old, small and vulnerable. One nest had two Great Egret eggs hatching simultaneously; in another nest there were three Snowy and two Great egret eggs. Still another had seven Great Egret eggs. In a Roseate Spoonbill nest four eggs were neatly arranged around a red and white fishing cork. Was this someone's joke or did the bird pick it up and put it there?

Opposite page:
A Tricolored Heron has selected this bush to be its home.

The Olivaceous Cormorants had mixed many heron and egret feathers with sticks and grass in the construction of their already whitewashed bowl-shaped nests. In each there were three to five eggs, but no young.

On South Deer Island the Tricolored Herons and White-faced Ibises had started laying their bright, Easter-egg-blue eggs. By hatching time these fade to a dull, washed-out blue. Their nests were mixed together in the low, scattered scrubby bushes and marsh grass. Nests of the two birds are very similar, both being stick platform affairs, but the ibises like to line their nests with grasses. The only way to positively tell which bird a nest belongs to is by egg size. The White-faced Ibis egg is larger, averaging 51.5 millimeters (2 inches) in length versus 44 millimeters (1.73 inches) for the Tricolored Heron egg.

Egg Development

Sandwich Terns lay single eggs, usually in shallow scrapes in the sand or shell, but sometimes don't bother digging a nest.

The egg is a most remarkable structure. Housed inside its thin shell are the developing chick, a food supply, two air supplies, and a waste disposal system. The only outside requirements for full development are warmth and oxygen.

When the egg is first laid, the yolk and white fill the shell completely. At this time the nascent chick is a small group of cells (blastoderm) lying on the yolk. The yolk and embryo are enclosed in the vitelline membrane, which keeps the yolk and egg white from mixing. The yolk, which supplies the food for the developing embryo, is made up of a mixture of proteins, fats, and carbohydrates. The albumen (white), which is about 88 percent water, 10 percent amino acids and minerals, provides moisture for the embryo and support for the yolk.

The eggshell is the protective enclosure for the developing chick. The shell is mostly calcium carbonate combined with small amounts of sodium chloride, magnesium, phosphate, and citric acid. Just inside the shell are two membranes which are fused together except at the blunt end, where they separate to form an air pocket. This is the air the chick will breathe just before hatching. Oxygen for the developing embryo diffuses in, and by-product carbon dioxide diffuses out through tiny pores in the eggshell.

During incubation the parent bird uses its bill to turn the egg several times every hour in order to stabilize the incu-bating temperature and to keep the embryo, which turns to stay in the upper part of the shell, from sticking to the shell. The yolk, being heavier, is always on the bottom.

Most birds wait to start incubating until the last egg in their clutch is laid so that all the chicks will be the same age and size. But the colonial birds start incubating when the first egg is laid, so the chicks hatch at different times, which accounts for the different sizes of the chicks in a nest. To develop normally, the egg must be kept just a few degrees below the parent bird's temperature of 104° F (40° C), ideally about 98 to 99° F, for the incubation period. According to *The Birder's Handbook,* the incubation period for Least Terns is twenty to twenty-two days; for American White Pelicans twenty-nine to thirty-six days; for most of the other colonial birds, twenty to thirty-one days.

In the first day after laying, the embryo's nervous system, digestive tract, and blood system start to form. By thirty-six hours the heart begins to beat, allowing the blood to carry food from the yolk through the newly developed veins to the devel-oping organs. On the second day the eyes, ears, aortal arches, and brain lobes begin to form. A thin sack, the amnion, begins to grow around the embryo on the third day, and by the fourth day completely encloses it. The amnion, found in birds, reptiles, and mammals, encloses the embryo in liquid, thus allowing reproduction to occur out of water. The head, eyes, and main blood vessels have formed, and the heart beats strongly.

During the second week the fetus grows rapidly, drawing food and moisture from the yolk and albumen. The air chamber develops at the blunt end of the egg as moisture evaporates from the egg and air diffuses between the two membranes that lie against the inner wall of the shell. The chick's wings and legs continue developing and down begins to form.

By 2½ weeks, the young chick completely fills the shell except for the air bubble and a small yolk sack. Before the chick hatches the yolk sac will be drawn through the umbilical opening into the young bird's body. This will provide the chick with food through the hatching process. The chick's initial moisture supply is provided by the amniotic fluid, which it has been swallowing for several days.

Finally, at about day twenty-one the chick is ready for its coming-out party. While it has been developing, the fetus has been growing a hatching muscle and an egg tooth. The hatching muscle is an enlarged muscle attached to the back of the head and neck; the egg tooth is an enlargement on the tip of the bill. The bill punctures the air chamber and the chick starts partially breathing with its lungs. Then, with its egg tooth against the inside of the shell, the chick uses its hatching muscle to provide the thrust to pip the shell. It struggles to free itself from its prison, using the egg tooth to break the shell all around: pushing, turning, breaking, resting—it is a mighty effort that can take several hours to two or three days. At last, however, the end of the shell falls away and the chick emerges. The hatching chick's persistent peeps switch the parents' behavior from incubating to nurturing the young.

A loose colony of Forster's Terns was nesting on the west side of the island on drifts of grass washed high in the marsh and on the shell bank. Some had already started laying eggs.

Two of the terns brought fish back to the colony, then strutted around holding the fish high until the females accepted them to seal their bond. I watched through my 800-millimeter lens while two other pairs went through their furious but brief mating ritual.

A group of Caspian Terns found the isolation they like on the west shell bank. Each pair was incubating one to three eggs in their scraped-out nests. The Caspian Tern's eggs, which are the same size as the Great Blue Heron's, 64.5 by 45 millimeters (2.54 by 1.77 inches), are very large relative to the tern's body size.

A week later, when I returned to Rollover Pass, a stiff northwesterly wind was blowing. I had to anchor on the southeast side of the larger of the islands and take a long, muddy wade to shore with the blind and camera gear.

The earliest of the Olivaceous Cormorant chicks were just hatching. Their plump, brownish bodies were completely naked, and their eyes were closed. Small heads waved randomly around on long skinny necks as the young birds squirmed in the nest.

More odd findings: Last week I ran across a Roseate Spoonbill nest with a fishing cork in it; this week I found one with an aerosol can and one with a beer can.

The Laughing Gulls were socializing, but there were no eggs yet. The Forster's Terns on the north marsh and one Great Blue Heron had laid and were incubating their eggs.

Back on North Deer Island the eggs of the early-nesting White Ibises on one hillside of the ridges were hatching. The chicks were covered with a black down. These four to five hundred nests were 1–3 feet off the ground in dense brush and prickly pear cactus. A later group with two to three hundred nests was on another hillside in a canebrake. The cane was broken down, and the smallish stick nests were on or near the ground. Each of these nests had one to three eggs almost identical to the Roseate Spoonbill's, chalky white with brown mottling, but slightly smaller. One surprise was that the birds don't just sit docilely on their nests but spend more of their time off the nests moving around the colony. Once in a while I heard a faint, guttural croak.

White Ibis

Eudocimus albus
FAMILY: THRESKIORNITHIDAE

A White Ibis stands guard over its eggs on Little Pelican Island.

The genus name *Eudocimus* is Latin taken from Greek words meaning "famous, in good standing, of high repute." *Albus* is Latin for "white" and refers to the plumage. The Old World ibis *Threskiornis aethiopica* was sacred to the Egyptians and can be traced back in their history some five thousand years. More than a million of the birds were mummified and buried with the pharaohs and in their own tombs in ancient Egypt. Brown curlew and other curlew variations (Spanish, stone, and white) were common names for the White Ibis.

White Ibises nest in fresh- and saltwater marshes and bays, always in colonies. They build substantial, well-cupped nests, 8 to 24 inches in diameter, from sticks, twigs, leaves, and sometimes Spanish moss, and add to them throughout the nesting season. The White Ibis prefers the warmer climates. It breeds from North Carolina to Florida, along the northern Gulf Coast, on both coasts of Mexico to northern South America, and is a year-round resident over most of its range. In the early days White Ibises were shot for food in the areas where they were plentiful.

Being social birds, the White Ibises are always found nesting, feeding, and traveling in flocks. In the mornings and evenings they can be seen flying to and from their feeding grounds, sometimes in diagonal lines, sometimes in loose undulating lines. Their flight is strong and determined with rapid wing strokes. The adults' pure white plumage, long downcurved bill, outstretched neck, and black wing tips serve as very good field marks. The black feathers on their wing tips have more pigment and so are stiffer and more wear resistant than the white feathers.

White Ibises prefer feeding in the shallow waters of small lakes, ponds, and fresh- and saltwater marshes. Their favorite foods are crawfish in freshwater areas and fiddler crabs around salt or brackish water. They also like cutworms, grasshoppers, and small water snakes.

Bent, in the *Life Histories of North American Marsh Birds*, quotes John James Audubon's (1840) description of the ingenuity this bird uses to catch food. Audubon described watching the ibis walk up to a crawfish mound, break off a piece of mud, and drop it down the crawfish's hole. The bird then took one step backward and waited. When the crawfish, responding to its instinct to clean its burrow, appeared at the entrance, the ibis seized it in its bill.

To cause minimal disturbance when I am looking for a place to photograph the colonies, I first stand off and study the area through my binoculars. Then I select a site for photographing on the edge of the colony, never in the middle, preferably with a south or west exposure for the best light. I always assemble my blind away from the nesting colony, often in the bow of my boat, carry it to the preselected site, stake it down, get my camera gear, and get inside. It's all done in two quick trips. This activity initially scares the parent birds off, but most return to their nests in five to fifteen minutes.

Late in the day I moved my blind into the marsh beside a shallow pool. Two Black-necked Stilts were feeding, a Blue-winged Teal was on its nest on the far bank, and White Ibises were gathering at the west end of the pool. Two first-year ibises joined the flock. A Great Blue Heron came and went while two Tricolored Herons came into the group, one walking within 6 feet of my blind. The ibises fed quietly in the shallows while several bathed themselves. The bathers lowered their bodies partially into the water, dipped their heads into the water, and rubbed their heads and beaks over as much of their bodies as they could reach. They ended the ritual by slightly spreading their wings, using them and their tails to splash water all over themselves. No wonder they always look so clean.

Finished for the day, I was walking down the shell bank to the boat when I found a dying Laughing Gull. I thought it was already gone but when I saw an eyelid move, I looked more closely. It did not appear to have the slightest hint of fear in its eyes. It seemed completely at peace and unafraid.

A few days later brought an incredible, absolutely bell-clear, blue-sky day. The temperature reached about 80° F. For several days before, strong northerly winds had pushed water out of the bay, causing extremely low tides. On this day, however, the winds had died to soft northerly breezes, and the water was glassy smooth.

Since the breeze was out of the northwest, I anchored on the east side of Little Pelican Island where, on a steep bank, the trees and bushes grow right to the edge of the water. White Ibis nests with eggs were in the nearby trees, and some 150 Tricolored Herons were nesting in bushes and on the ground.

Snowy Egrets were in some distant bushes. I kept my distance because Great-tailed Grackles live here, too. Whenever the herons and ibises are scared off their nests, the grackles move in and destroy the eggs.

Later, the wind shifted to the southwest, so I moved the boat to a place on the west shell bank where there is never any nesting. A "splattering" of gulls was standing along the bank, but there were no nests. One hundred fifty White-faced Ibises were building their platform nests out in the marsh grass. I didn't see them when I approached in the boat, but when the gulls sounded the alarm I saw their heads pop up over the grass. A group of Black Skimmers was staking out an area where the shell bank joins a large salt marsh. There were no eggs, but a half-dozen depressions in the broken oyster shell signaled the skimmers' intent to nest. This was very heartening because the year before there were just a few Black Skimmers nesting in the bay area. As I walked along I heard the unmistakable peep-peep of a pair of American Oystercatchers circling out over the water. An oystercatcher never leads you back to its nest; it just keeps walking and circling.

Out on the sand flats, well away from the water, a group of Royal Terns was nesting and had already laid a dozen eggs. This is the earliest I had seen Royal Tern eggs.

On the way back to the dock, I went by Down Deer Spoil Island, a small, low-lying island adjacent to North Deer Island, and a popular Caspian Tern nesting place. The Caspians had it to themselves except for a few gulls and a pair of oystercatchers. I didn't go ashore but just drifted in and watched from the boat. Through my binoculars I could see twenty-one nests with eggs and, of those, fourteen had two eggs.

Three days later, Pat Gerlach, a talented wildlife photographer from North Dakota, and I set up blinds in a grassy clearing on the west side of the egret nesting area at Rollover Pass. From there we had good mid- and late-day light for photographing the Great Egrets, Great Blue Herons, Roseate Spoonbills, Olivaceous Cormorants, Snowy Egrets, and the ever-elusive Black-crowned Night-Herons.

All the egret nests that I saw had eggs, and in some were newly hatched chicks. These birds pack every available space with nests, then spend the rest of the season defending their little territories. A cormorant, sitting on its eggs in a nearby nest to the right of the blind, didn't just docilely go to sleep but was always alert, turning right, left, watching, jabbing at any bird flying too close. When a Great Blue Heron landed beside the cormorant, it made a couple of vigorous lunges at the much larger heron and succeeded in persuading it to move to the next bush.

Roseate Spoonbill

Ajaia ajaja (Linnaeus)
FAMILY: THRESKIORNITHIDAE

Both *Ajaia* and *ajaja* come from the Brazilian Indian name for the bird. The origin is unknown. The term *roseate* is for the splash of rosy red on the wings and the pink plumage. Nuttall refers to the birds as the red or American spoonbills. In the mid-1800's the Floridians called them pink curlews. Another common name was rosy spoonbill. The name *spoonbill* refers to the wide, flat shape of the bill. Because of the spoonbills' overall pink color with splashes of red on the wings, some people of the Gulf Coast still call them flamingoes.

Roseate Spoonbills are strictly coastal birds, preferring the bays and salt marshes, but wanderers are sometimes seen in freshwater marshes and along river systems. In the United States the spoonbills breed along the Texas and southwest Louisiana coasts and in southern Florida. They also breed in Cuba and Mexico south through Central and South America to northern Argentina. Roseate Spoonbill nests, constructed of sticks and lined with twigs, leaves, and grass, are well-built, deeply cupped structures. The birds' favorite nesting places are in low trees and bushes, but they will also nest on the ground. The spoonbill eggs are about 66 millimeters (2.6 inches) long, dirty white, with brown spots or blotches. On small islands, like the Rollover Pass Islands, young spoonbills leave their nests at about six weeks and gather along the shoreline, where they learn to fly and feed themselves. On large islands, like North Deer or Little Pelican, where the nests are in large trees or dense brush, the chicks must stay in their nests until fledging time.

When John James Audubon visited Galveston in 1837, there were thousands of spoonbills on the Texas Gulf Coast, but by the early 1900's the plumers had reaped such destruction that only a scattering of breeding birds remained. The reason for the excessive extermination was a simple matter of money. In 1858 an observer visiting Pelican Island on the Indian River (Florida) reported that the plumers were killing up to sixty birds per day. The wings were being sent to St. Augustine to be sold as fans for the ladies (never mind that fans could have been made out of any number of other materials). The gunners never cared about the future of the bird, just about making a quick profit. Bent tells us that the destruction was so complete that as late as 1920 a party consisting of T. G. Pearson and Mr. and Mrs. W. L. Finley was able to find

Opposite page:
Roseate Spoonbills and other birds, returning from feeding in the nearby bays, stop for a short rest before returning to their nests.

only 179 spoonbills, all on the upper Texas coast. In 1923 a party including A. C. Bent himself found just one ibis-spoonbill rookery on the Texas coast. It took them four days of watching the flight lines to and from feeding grounds to finally find the rookery in a deep swamp along the Guadalupe River in Victoria County.

Since then the spoonbills have recovered and as of 1980 there were two thousand pairs nesting along the Texas coast. They are for the most part quiet, sociable, serious-minded birds. I saw one give a sound thrashing to a Snowy Egret that apparently had invaded the spoonbill's territory. The spoonbill jumped on top and pecked the snowy until it could wriggle free and make its escape. Spoonbills mix their nests randomly with those of herons and egrets but gather into flocks to feed. While the half-dozen-to-several-hundred-member flock feeds, one or more birds will act as sentinels so that they are virtually impossible to approach.

What they display in their physical beauty they completely lack in their songmaking ability. The only voice I have heard was a very low, almost inaudible croak while the parent was on a nest tending to its chick.

In flight, the spoonbills form diagonal lines or inverted V's like geese. They fly with their heads and necks outstretched, beaks pointing straight forward as though they know where they want to go.

Great Egrets and Great Blue Herons always engage in greeting rituals when joining their mates on the nest. The returning bird squawks while on its final approach, and when it lands, both birds ruffle their neck and head feathers, engage in friendly sparring, and squawk at each other in a recognition communication. Great Blue Herons sit on their nests like statues for what seems like hours without moving a feather. The Great Egrets were more active, sitting for a few minutes, moving around, shifting the eggs around, settling down, getting up, and changing positions. The Snowy Egrets weren't doing much incubating, just walking around fussing with the other birds. An Olivaceous Cormorant came back to

the nest carrying a stick, went through the same greeting ritual, then gave the stick to its mate, who placed it in the nest.

About mid-afternoon we moved to Little Pelican Island, where instead of working from blinds we stayed in the open just outside nesting area perimeters. Pat was intently watching two Roseate Spoonbills in the top of a nearby tree through his 500-millimeter lens. He noticed that they were building their nest with some "borrowed" materials. One was standing at the edge of its nest, the other on a branch next to the nest. The second spoonbill was removing sticks from a neighbor's nest and giving them one by one to its mate, which was using them to weave its own nest.

On the higher ground on North Deer Island, prickly pear thickets, brush, and trees provide a variety of nesting sites. The remains of last year's nests, seen in these trees, will be the starting structures for this year's nests.

The coastal environment has changed drastically in the past one hundred years, and the human population projections for the future show a continuous increase. The colonial birds and even the managed game species such as ducks and geese are being squeezed into smaller and smaller areas. We don't have the large mammals on the Gulf and lower Atlantic coasts that are so popular with tourists in other parts of the country. What we do have are large populations of some of the most beautiful birds in the world, and very little public money is spent in supporting or protecting them. What can compare with a Roseate Spoonbill in its full adult plumage, or a Snowy Egret? As serious as the killing for the millinery trade was in the late 1800's and early 1900's, the effects of the killings were not irreversible because some birds survived and their habitat was not destroyed. Once the killing had stopped there was ample wilderness in which the birds could nest undisturbed and replenish their populations.

Today the threat is more insidious and much more serious. Many of the islands the birds are nesting on now are spoil islands, that is, islands that were created by the material that was dug out during the building of the Intracoastal Waterway. These islands became the salvation of the birds as they were displaced from historical nesting sites on the beaches and coastal swamps and marshes by human population pressures. The spoil itself was a heavy clay, and most islands are fairly stable. In the long run, however, the water will win and reclaim many of these islands. The silt material dredged out during the routine maintenance of the waterway is too light to use for building new islands, and some, like the Vingt-et-un Islands (NAS sanctuaries) are washing away, subsiding into the bays, or, like Redfish Island, being overrun with people. The alarming fact is that there has been a significant net decrease in quality nesting and feeding habitat in the past fifteen years. It is up to us to respect the wilderness areas the birds and animals require and to prevent further deterioration of their habitat from occurring.

Black-crowned
Night-Heron

Nycticorax nycticorax
FAMILY: ARDEIDAE

*The Black-crowned
Night-Heron surveys
the territory before
going to its nest.*

Nycticorax is the Latin spelling of the Greek *nyktikorax,* "night raven," which is formed from *nyx, nyctos,* "night," and *korax,* "raven." Nuttall refers to them as qua-birds and kwah-birds. Other common names include American night-heron, night-heron, quawk, quok, and squawk.

The Black-crowned Night-Heron is readily identified by its black crown and back, black bill, and grayish neck and wings. This stocky heron is at home in fresh as well as salt or brackish water. A truly cosmopolitan bird, it breeds in south central and southeast Canada, throughout most of the United States, and south to Tierra del Fuego. It is also found in eastern and southern Europe, southern Russia, Iran, Africa, Madagascar, India, China, Indochina, and Indonesia.

True to its name, it is largely nocturnal, roosting during the day, moving off to feeding grounds around dusk, and returning to its roost at dawn. These herons are social birds and mix their nests in with the other herons and egrets. On Little Pelican Island there are about two hundred breeding pairs, although they are difficult to count because their nests are scattered in a dense, bushy area; I count the birds perched on the bushes above their nests to try to estimate the total number. Getting a more accurate count would require combing the area by wading back and forth through the brush, an activity which would result in the disturbance of many of the nests in the area.

There does not seem to be such a thing as a "typical" Black-crowned Night-Heron nest. They are willing to work with whatever materials and sites are available. The ones I have seen on the Gulf Coast have been primitive stick plat-forms deep in the bushes and scrubby trees. A. C. Bent (1926) found them "nesting in tall canes, where their nests were made wholly of the stems of dead canes. On Dressing Point, in Matagorda Bay (Texas), we found a fair-sized colony nesting on the dry ground among tufts of tall grass." A few lines later, "W. L. Finley (1906) found a colony of about 200 pairs in a fir forest south of Portland, Oregon, in which none of the nests were less than 130 feet up and some were 160 feet above the ground. In a colony which he found at the lower end of San Francisco Bay, California, in the summer of 1904, he noted 41 nests of the Great Blue Heron and 28 nests of the Black-crowned Night-Heron in a single giant sycamore, 7 feet thick at the base, 120 feet high and with a spread equal to its height."

An unfortunate incident in relation to the Black-crowned Night-Herons taught me a lesson that I will pass on for the benefit of other photographers and observers. I was photo-graphing Great Egret and Great Blue Heron nests from the permanent blind I had built earlier in the season. From this strange looking "tree" that the birds had accepted and were roosting on, I could easily see into the heron and egret nests, but the night-herons presented a problem. Their nests were deep inside the bushes and difficult to observe, let alone photograph. But there was one nest with three eggs, about 2 feet off the ground, which was in a perfect position—except for a few tree limbs, which I removed. I looked forward to getting some unimpeded shots, but unfortunately, on my next trip to the blind I was dismayed to find that the only thing I had accomplished by cutting the tree was to give a predator easy access to the nest. It was totally destroyed and all the eggs were gone. Since then I have been extremely reluctant to "improve" visual access to the nests.

On another trip to Little Pelican Island I set up my blind on the north end of the island on the edge of a colony of more than one hundred nesting Black-crowned Night-Herons. At any time there were thirty heads peering over the tops of the bushes. I could have found some by bulling my way into the brush, but the sacrifice in destroyed nests would be too great. One landed on a bush 15 to 20 feet away and looked right, left, over, and under, spending fifteen to twenty minutes making sure its secret was secure. It stepped to a lower branch, went through the whole security check again, and the last glimpse I had was of it walking on the ground through the brush to its nest. I didn't succeed in photographing any Black-crowned Night-Herons on their nests.

I folded up my blind and walked out to the flats where the Laughing Gulls would be nesting. They were all overhead. The sky was clear, but I seemed to be in a rainstorm. I caught a few direct hits, but fortunately the gulls' aim is not very precise.

A small group of Sandwich Terns on the sand flats had eggs. I was standing within 30 feet of them, and they were squawking but staying right on their eggs. Fifty eggs lay within a 10-foot-diameter circle. Along the shell bank, I counted six separate groups of the Royal and Sandwich terns; the early ones had eggs. More birds were arriving daily; before the season ended, more than ten thousand terns were nesting here. Until the early 1980's there were no terns except a few Forster's nesting on the island. Then suddenly the Royal and Sandwich

Feeding time with all the herons and egrets, like this Reddish Egret, involves a wrestling match. Grasping the beak by the young bird stimulates the parent's feeding reflex.

terns took a fancy to Little Pelican Island and this shell bank in particular, and each year since there has been a mixed cacophony of seven to twelve thousand birds nesting here.

On the way back to the dock, I went by South Deer Island to check on the Caspian Terns. I stopped the engine, drifted in close, and scanned the nests with binoculars. All the adults took off to come out to greet me. Three of the fifty nests had chicks; most others had eggs; latecomers were just digging fresh nests.

Twenty-knot southeasterly winds, gusting to 25–30, made for a rough, wet boat ride on the next trip to Little Pelican Island. I've found that the best way to carry my camera gear in these conditions is in foam-padded ice chests. It was too windy to set up my blind in the open areas, so I just moved around and did some observing.

More Black Skimmers had joined this first skimmer colony on the shell bank where the bank joins salt marsh. With the exception of the previous year, the skimmers had nested right here every year since I had been coming to this island. Some of the one hundred pairs had one to three eggs in their nests; others were just digging their little scrapes and settling in. Another group of skimmers established itself about 400 yards down the shell bank to the southwest in an area where I had never seen any nesting before.

The Laughing Gulls were building nests. I walked all the way across the sand flats where some two thousand gulls were gathered and after looking in over one hundred nests finally found one egg.

The White-faced Ibises had completed their platform nests out in the marsh and most contained one to three of their blue to greenish-blue eggs. Some of the eggs had been pecked open, and I hurried on so the parent birds could return to their nests before the gulls destroyed any more eggs. The ibises haven't figured out that they have to guard their nests every minute against the predatory gulls. I didn't go back there until I was sure the ibis eggs had hatched.

Hail, bounteous May, that dost inspire
  Mirth and youth and warm desire.
(MILTON, "ON MAY MORNING," 1629 – 1630)

Hatching and Chicks

MAY

In the month of May, the birds' nesting season is approaching its peak. The chicks from the earliest nests are almost grown; some will be leaving their nests. The majority of the breeding birds are incubating eggs or rearing young. Some late nesters will be just arriving in the colony to build nests and lay their eggs. May is a busy time in the colony. Nests require constant maintenance. Young birds demand to be fed regularly, so the parents make frequent round trips to and from nearby feeding grounds.

In early May I went to Rollover Pass to get some pictures of Olivaceous Cormorants feeding their chicks. I set my blind in an open area where I could see into three nests. Each of the nests, on low bushes about 2 feet off the ground, had three chicks. One set of chicks looked to be two to three weeks old, the second set seven to ten days old, and the third just one to three days old. The youngest chicks' eyes were closed, and they were totally naked. The oldest set were the first to be fed. They didn't grasp their parents' bills for a wrestling match like herons and egrets but stretched their necks to their full height (their necks make up more than half of their body length) and rapidly vibrated their heads against the parents' necks or heads. Parents often have a problem catching this rapidly moving target, but when the parent is ready to feed, it opens its bill,

Opposite page:
Caspian Terns prefer
their own nesting sites
on isolated shell banks
or sand bars, like this
one on South Deer
Island. Those too close
to the water sometimes
get washed away in
storms or high tides.

starts the chick's head down its throat, and lowers its head until the chick is buried to its shoulders in the parent's gullet.

The parents took turns sitting with the youngest chicks all through the day and fed them every twenty to forty minutes. The chicks wanted to be fed, but their heads just waved blindly around like a clown out of a jack-in-the-box on those long, skinny necks. The parent's job was to gently catch this bobbing head and guide it into its throat. I watched as the chick's head disappeared and could see its body convulsing as it gulped down the food. When its head emerged, it was covered to the shoulders with the slimy, fishy soup. Along with the soup the parent regurgitated some solid pieces onto the nest and, after feeding, picked them up to make more fish soup.

One of the parents of the week-old chicks sat unresponsively on the nest all day long. Chicks on the other nests had been fed, but not these. Finally, in the late afternoon the parent fed one of its chicks and was quickly set upon by the others but, instead of feeding, walked to the far edge of the nest. One of the begging chicks was in the way, but its parent just walked gently over it, stood on the edge of the nest, then jumped off, knocking the nestling off the nest as well. I thought to myself "There's a dead chick," but kept the lens trained on the nest. After a few minutes I saw a little head reappear over the edge of the nest. It was using its beak to pull itself up; then one wing appeared, and the other wing, until finally it was back on the nest. Had this nest been in a tree, where most cormorants nest, the chick certainly would have died.

A nearby Great Blue Heron with two seven-to-ten-day-old chicks sat on its nest, hardly moving for three to four hours. When ready, it stepped onto the nest, slowly lowered its head, held it near the chicks for a minute or two, then regurgitated several fish that were snapped up as fast as the chicks could swallow them.

When I went to Swan Lake four days later, there were seventy to one hundred Black Skimmer nests, eight to twelve Gull-billed Tern nests, and about forty Forster's Tern nests in a 75-yard space. The nests of the Gull-billed Terns were scattered in with and are much like those of the skimmers, shallow scrapes in the shell, except that the Gull-billed Terns often arrange a few twigs or grass blades around their nests. Their eggs look very much like those of the Forster's Terns, brownish with black mottling, but are slightly larger. The Forster's Terns also mixed some nests in with the skimmers', but put much more effort into building their stick and grass structures on the backside of the shell bank and on grass drifts and debris in the marsh grass.

Gull-billed Tern

Sterna nilotica
FAMILY: LARIDAE

Tern derives from a group of Scandinavian words—Norwegian *terna,* Danish *terne,* Old Norse *therna,* and Swedish *tarna,* meaning "sea swallow." The terms *starn* and *stern* were used in some Old English dialects. Choate, in *The Dictionary of American Bird Names* (1985), tells us that in 1544, W. Turner Latinized *stern, starn,* or *tern* from the Anglo-Saxon *stearn* to *sterna.* It is now used for the genus name. Until 1983 the Latin

This Gull-billed Tern chick is learning to fly and will soon be self-supporting.

name was *Gelochelidon nilotica*. The term *Gelochelidon* was made by combining the Greek *gelos*, "laughter," and *khelidon*, "swallow," for "laughing swallow." The species name is the feminine of the Latin *niloticus* for the type specimen found near the Nile. The common name is for the stubby black bill which resembles a gull's bill. Other common names have included marsh tern, Anglican tern, Egyptian tern, Nile tern, and Nuttall's tern.

The Gull-billed Tern is light gray above, white below, with a black crown that extends over its head and down the back of its neck. It breeds on the Salton Sea, California, along the Gulf Coast from Texas to Florida; and on the Atlantic Coast north to New Jersey. It also breeds in the West Indies, Mexico, Central America, and along the Atlantic Coast of South America to northern Argentina. Most Gull-billeds nest in salt-water habitats, but some find suitable nesting around fresh-water marshes and waterways. In the Old World, they live in the British Islands, parts of Europe, and northern Africa.

Some early writers, including Nuttall, referred to this bird as the marsh tern for its preference for feeding in the salt marsh, seldom in the open bays, and in some places using the marsh for a breeding ground. Nuttall said the terns "keep apart by themselves" and told of their nesting on the drift grasses around the salt marsh and "preparing no artificial nest." Bent and other observers saw them nesting on the sandy Virginia and Carolina beaches in the company of Black Skimmers and Common Terns. I have only seen them on the shell banks of small islands associating with Black Skimmers, Forster's Terns, Laughing Gulls, and occasionally Least Terns. The Gull-billed's nest is a scrape in the shell or sand much like the skimmer's but with a few twigs deposited around the perimeter.

In the 1800's the Gull-billeds came under attack on two fronts. People collected their eggs for food, and gunners shot them for the millinery trade. Bent's *Life Histories of North American Gulls and Terns* gives some population figures for Cobb's Island (Virginia) that show the effects of this combined onslaught. By 1890 the population was decreasing, but the bird was described as "common at Cobb's Island, and breeds, formerly in great abundance." By 1900 the population "had been reduced to about a thousand," in 1901 to three hundred, in 1903 only eight pairs were found, and in 1907 A. C. Bent found only two pairs though there were a few others scattered on surrounding islands. By 1911 the population had climbed to eight pairs, and after protection was established in the early 1920's, the population increased again, but never fully recovered from its virtual extermination. At present, Gull-billed Terns are widespread but uncommon and may be declining in numbers over their range.

I set my blind on the edge of the shell bank to photograph the terns, and if the tide had come in, I would have been in the water. On the nest closest to me a Gull-billed was incubating two eggs while its mate just hung around the nest. Little or no interaction took place between them, but this may have been its way of keeping its mate company. The other nests I could see had only one egg each. I would be back later to check the progress of this colony.

About a thousand White Ibises were nesting in a dense thicket of head-high bushes mixed with prickly pear cactus on one of the ridges on North Deer Island. I walked in the marsh along the edge of the nesting area and looked into a few nests. All the eggs had hatched, and the chicks I saw appeared to be one to two weeks old.

A week later, back on North Deer Island, four Great Blue Heron nests, in trees 6 to 12 feet high, had chicks that were 15–18 inches tall. Also in the bushes and trees around me were Great and Snowy egrets, Roseate Spoonbills, Tricolored Herons, and Black-crowned Night-Herons. The spoonbills have the loudest wingbeats of any of the birds here. I listened for the whump-whump beat of their wings against the air as they flew by.

A spoonbill perched on a branch beside a Great Blue Heron nest while the heron was absent. The heron returned, stood on its nest for at least an hour paying no heed to the spoonbill, then suddenly squawked and thrust its bill at the spoonbill, forcing it to leave. The heron was ready to feed its young and gently lowered its head to the young birds' level so they could go through the ritual of grasping the parent's beak and wrestling for their food. The fish worked its way up the parent's throat, was regurgitated, and was downed immediately by the youngster who stood there with a "Where's the rest of it?" look on its face. At feeding time the young ones become very animated—squawking, flapping, moving around the nest, sparring with rival siblings, grabbing each other's beaks, and nipping at their parents' legs. The young birds' day consists of hours and hours of rest interspersed with brief moments of frenzied feeding.

Parents were staying near the nest but were not spending much time caring for the chicks, since they were feathered and could tolerate the midday heat. One of the adult herons returned to the nest from a fishing trip and tried to feed its young a fish that was too large, so the parent downed it again. Two more hours of those powerful digestive juices were required before the nestling could swallow the fish.

One of the adult Great Blue Herons came back to its nest and joined its mate in their noisy greeting ritual. These large herons have a low guttural croak, but it is the Olivaceous Cormorants that have the deepest voice—they definitely sing bass in the bird colony.

The young cormorants on the nest at Rollover Pass in front of the blind were one-quarter grown, completely covered with down, and growing fast. Less than two weeks before, they had been totally naked, with their eyes closed. Their attentive parent stood over the nest with wings spread for over an hour, shading the chicks. The chicks were not interested in feeding, but, instead, burrowed under the parent to get out of the sun. Finally, it looked as if they wanted to feed. They begged for a minute, quit, then tried to burrow under the parent again. All three could not find shade simultaneously, so it was a matter of pushing and shoving, the one in the sun pushing a shaded one out, each getting a little bit of shade this way.

Right next door, another cormorant nest that last week held four eggs now contained four naked chicks. The parents took turns with the babysitting duties, shaded the chicks from the sun, and every so often fed them a runny fish soup.

A Great Egret stood over its nest shading its chicks, one a day or two old, the other just hatched and still wet. Their heads barely showed above the edge of the nest. The parent lowered its head and regurgitated a half-dozen tiny, well-digested fish beside the chicks. Both chicks pecked at the fish, but even at this age the older chick took time out for a few jabs at the still-wet one. The mother watched the feeding and picked up and swallowed the leftover bits of fish.

In the previous week there had been no nests in the grassy area to the left of my blind. This week a group of late-nesting Forster's Terns and a few Laughing Gulls had established nests. Also, some new Tricolored Heron nests were down inside some knee-high bushes.

The male sat with the older cormorant chicks for four hours; then the female returned. She was ready to feed, and the young birds sensed it. She fed two of the chicks, then pulled away. She was keeping track and stepped over the two more aggressive chicks to feed the left-out third one.

American White Pelican

Pelecanus erythrorhynchos
FAMILY: PELECANIDAE

On South Bird Island in Laguna Madre, two American White Pelicans are incubating their eggs.

Pelecanus comes from the Greek *pelekus* or "axe." In *The Birds*, Aristophanes uses the word for both a pelican type water bird and a woodpecker. The designation was used for birds with prominent bills, as Turner in 1544 used the term *pelecanus* for a spoonbill. *Erythrorhynchos* is derived from the Greek *erythros,* "red," and *rhynchos,* "beak," thus meaning "red-beaked." The name refers to the reddish tint of the bill during the breeding season. Common names have included white pelican, common pelican, and rough-billed pelican.

American White Pelicans are white with black primary and outer secondary feathers. They are at home in both fresh and salt water, wintering on the southern California, northern Gulf of Mexico, and Florida coasts south to Nicaragua and nesting mainly on inland freshwater lakes. They breed on islands in western Canada and the northwestern United States, east to Minnesota and south to northern California and Colorado. There is also a small breeding colony on the central Texas coast in the Laguna Madre in Kleberg County. American White Pelicans nest on the ground, sometimes on bare ground in small depressions, or on built-up mounds of dirt and debris.

During the winter the breeding birds grow a fin-shaped horn in about the center of the upper bill; the horn falls off midway through the nesting season. Pelicans lay one to three eggs, most commonly two, but only the oldest chick normally survives. Both parents share responsibility during the one-month incubation period, after which the young pelicans hatch blind, naked, and helpless. For the first couple of weeks the chicks are fed a regurgitated fishy soup by the parent, which gently guides the small chick's head with the tip of its bill and regurgitates the soup into the lower end of its pouch. Young birds are excellent swimmers from the time they leave the nest and, since white pelicans feed while floating on the water, learn to feed themselves before they learn to fly at about two months.

With a nine-foot wingspan, American White Pelicans are among the largest birds in North America, and although they look awkward on land, they are strong swimmers and fliers. Cruising just a few feet off the water, they alternate powerful wing beats with long glides, during which they seem not to lose an inch of altitude. They fly to and from feeding grounds in echelon or V formation like geese. A most thrilling experience is witnessing the birds leaving the coast for the spring migration or returning in the fall. A swirling mass of the great white birds may be seen high against the blue sky, looping, soaring, circling, riding the thermals, seldom flapping, like a silent aerial ballet.

When the young birds are about one-third grown, they become more independent and wander around the nesting island with their peers. About this time feeding becomes much more active. W. L. Finley observed an extraordinary feeding sequence in 1907 (recorded in Bent 1922). Finley described how the youngster fell on the ground, flapping its wings as if it were starving, in front of the adult bird. This failing, the chick got up and started pecking at its mother's beak, with more success. The mother opened her beak, allowing the youngster to bury its head all the way to its wings in her throat, where it remained buried for a full two minutes, eating everything within reach. The mother finally succeeded in dislodging it by "shaking back and forth. The mother shook around over 10 or 12 feet of ground till she literally swung the young bird off his feet and sent him sprawling over the dry tules."

A parent Great Blue Heron brought back an 8-inch fish to its two-to-three-week-old chicks. One young bird gulped it down whole and wound up standing around for an hour with the fish's tail sticking out of its beak before managing to swallow it.

In mid-May I went to Corpus Christi to see the American White Pelicans nesting in Laguna Madre and the Brown Pelicans nesting in Corpus Christi Bay. Both islands are NAS sanctuaries, so I made arrangements to be accompanied by Ray Little, the warden in charge.

It was a long boat ride to South Bird Island but well worth the time. As we approached, we could see the mass of white pelicans covering the higher part of the island. We anchored the boat and waded around the island. The pelicans were new to me, so I took directions from Ray. It turned out that the same techniques of moving slowly, being patient, and taking time worked as well for the pelicans as for the other birds. When I saw their heads come up in alarm, I just stopped until they relaxed. I worked my way in close enough so that one bird completely filled the frame with the 800-millimeter lens. These are enormous birds! I estimated that there were 350 of these always peaceful, social birds crowded together on a small part of the island, leaving just enough space between nests to allow access for the adult birds. White pelicans, nesting on the ground, are not great nest builders, fashioning small hollows in the grass or scratching out shallow depressions in the bare dirt. The early chicks were about one-third grown, but most were not old enough to wander very far and were standing around the nests with the parents. Early nesting pelicans had established nests on the east side of the island, and this is where the older chicks were. As we moved around to the west side of the island, where the late arrivals were, we didn't see any chicks, only parents sitting on eggs.

This is a very unusual island. Not only is it the only white pelican nesting area within 1,000 miles, but a mixed colony of a thousand Royal, Sandwich, and Caspian terns was nesting around a small lagoon. Ray asked me to verify that Caspians were indeed mixed in with the other terns. I was lucky enough to get a photograph of Royal and Caspian terns sitting side by side on nests. According to the books, the Caspians prefer not to mix with the others.

After another long boat ride up Laguna Madre into Corpus Christi Bay, we saw the Brown Pelicans doing their spectacular feeding dives from 15 to 40 feet. On Pelican Island the Brown Pelicans built stick nests in the scrubby bushes 1–2 feet off the ground. Forty or so were standing on the bank just in front of the nesting area. When we approached with the boat, the ones at the edge of the water moved 100 yards farther on and settled down again, but the birds that were on their nests stayed put. I watched two of the parents feed their chicks in the same style as the cormorants—with the baby's head disappearing down the parent's gullet—while the parent of a very young chick gently guided its baby's head into the lower tip of its pouch so that it could have some regurgitated fish.

Back in Galveston Bay, Redfish Island, a spoil island built from dredged materials from the construction of the Houston Ship Channel, is washed and continuously reshaped by strong tides and ships' wakes. On the north end was a loose colony of two hundred Black Skimmers, forty Forster's Terns, and what

I really came to see, twenty Least Terns. I also saw one Gull-billed Tern flying by. The Least Terns had their nests spread 3 to 10 feet apart on the northern tip of the island, which is made up of large, broken oyster shell. The tiny, speckled eggs, laid in ready-made hollows in the oyster shell, were almost impossible to see. I unfolded a small camp stool, set my tripod low, and within minutes the terns were back sitting on their nests, some within about 25 feet.

Brown Pelican

Pelecanus occidentalis
FAMILY: PELECANIDAE

Occidentalis means "western," from the Latin *occidere,* "to fall or set," as in the setting of the sun. Brown is the bird's predominant color. Other common names have included American brown pelican and common pelican.

Brown Pelicans incubate their eggs on large stick nests about a foot off the ground in this nesting area in Corpus Christi Bay.

Adult Brown Pelicans have grayish-brown bodies with white or sometimes yellow heads and necks. With its 4-foot length and 7-foot wingspan, the Brown Pelican is the smallest of the pelican family. Unlike the American White Pelican, the Brown is strictly coastal, seldom straying inland. The breeding range extends from the coasts of southern California and of North Carolina south to Florida, both coasts of Mexico, the West Indies, Venezuela, and Chile. The Browns build substantial platform nests on the ground, on bushes, or in trees, using sticks, grass, leaves, or other available materials. Brown Pelicans lay two to four eggs, and the parents share incubation duties for about one month. Chicks in treetop nests stay on the nest for about two months, while those on the ground stay on the nest for just over one month. Brown Pelicans dive for their food, which takes practice, so the parents continue to feed their offspring after they have fledged while the young birds sharpen their hunting skills.

The state bird of Louisiana, Brown Pelicans formerly bred abundantly on the Texas and Louisiana coasts—Louisiana at one time had fifty thousand, but by 1962 had none. The Texas population also took a sharp plunge in the mid-1950's, and in California only five young Brown Pelicans were raised in the whole state in 1969. The reason for the population collapse was traced to the pesticides DDT and dieldrin, both of which were concentrating in the marine food chain. The DDT interfered with the birds' calcium metabolism and caused them to lay thin-shelled eggs which resulted in breakage.

At present the California, South Carolina, and Florida populations seem to be either recovering or stable, even though their eggshells are still slightly thinner than before the advent of DDT. Brown Pelicans are on the endangered species lists in Texas and Louisiana, but the populations are recovering in both states. Breeding colonies have worked their way from the lower to the central Texas coast and, at this writing, are breeding as far north as Matagorda County. Brown Pelicans are commonly seen on Galveston Bay, but as yet, none are nesting there.

A female Least Tern, standing out on the edge of the shell bank, was being courted by a male, who was trying to offer her a tiny, silvery fish. With his offering, he walked up to her while shaking his head from side to side, but she didn't accept the fish, so he turned and walked away. She turned and followed him, so he turned back to entice her some more. Although he didn't succeed this time, as she wasn't quite ready, they would probably soon be mating and starting a family.

Least Tern

Sterna antillarum
FAMILY: LARIDAE

The Least Tern established its nest in the large broken oyster shell on Redfish Island. This island has since eroded away.

The Least Tern started out as *Sterna antillarum*, then was changed to *S. albifrons*. In 1983 its name was changed back to *antillarum* to differentiate it from the Little Tern, *S. albifrons*, which is found only in the Old World. The name *antillarum* is from the modern Latin, meaning "of the Antilles," for the area where the species was first described. *Albifrons* was derived from *albus,* "white," and *frons,* "forehead": "white forehead" for the white stripe starting above the eyes and going across the forehead. *Least* is for the birds' small size. Actually this is not the smallest of the terns; the Damara, *Sterna balaenarum,* of southwestern Africa has an inch shorter wingspan. Other common names for the Least Tern include silvery tern, little striker, lesser tern, little tern, minute tern, sea swallow, and silver ternlet.

The Least Tern has virtual worldwide distribution, but two subspecies, the California and Interior, are on the U.S. Fish and Wildlife Service's list of endangered species in North America as being "in danger of extinction throughout all or a significant portion of its range." In the United States the Least Tern breeds from northern California to Mexico, all along the Gulf Coast, and from southern Maine to the Florida Keys. It is primarily coastal, though the Interior subspecies follows the river valleys inland and nests on the sandbars along the Mississippi, Red, Platte, Ohio, Missouri, and Colorado river systems. The Least Tern also ranges south to Peru and Brazil. In the Old World it ranges from the Baltic seacoast through the Mediterranean, Black, and Caspian seas, along the West African coast, and across the Indian Ocean to India, Burma, the Philippines, Sumatra, Japan, and Korea.

The Least Tern's nest consists of a simple scrape in the sand or shell, sometimes lined with a few pebbles or broken shell, sometimes not. Nuttall once said that these terns let the sun do the incubating and sit on the eggs only at night and during inclement weather. This is not true. Both parents share the incubation duties, and I have photographed them incubating on bright, sunny days. They were the last to abandon the overrun beaches for the more secure nesting sites on the spoil islands after trying to adjust to civilization. Oberholser tells of their laying eggs in the heel prints left by fishermen's boots. Like the Caspians, the Least Terns are not sociable and prefer their own private colony.

The Least, Gull-billed, and Common terns suffered along with the egrets in the quest to satisfy the needs of the millinery trade. While not sociable, the Least Terns are very tame, and this trait cost them dearly in the late 1800's. During the nesting season they gather into small areas, so that shooting them was no challenge at all. Whole colonies were exterminated in a single season. As each bird fell, the gunners in effect killed all its descendants forever.

In 1921, A. C. Bent quoted a series of eyewitness accounts of the slaughter that took place along the East Coast of the United States from New Jersey to Florida in the late nineteenth and early twentieth centuries. He reported that professional hunters, joined by local fishermen and oystermen, shot up to 1,200 birds a day along the Virginia coast alone and as many as 100,000 in a single season to supply the millinery trade. Gunners received ten to twelve cents per bird, not a bad wage at the time!

When Alexander Wilson (1766–1813), the "father of American ornithology," visited the Cape May, New Jersey, beaches, the Least Terns were abundant and "flew in clouds around him." Bent (1921) quoted G. S. Morris, who described seeing two millinery hunters on the same beaches in the summer of 1885. Morris wrote that they had two piles about knee-high of Least and Common terns, which they were sending to New York City, and for which they were to receive twelve cents apiece.

Frank Chapman visited Cobb's Island (Virginia) in 1902 to gather material for his habitat group and found the Least Terns completely gone. In 1903 he wrote that the former captain of a lifesaving station told him that as many as 1,400 Least Terns had been killed in one day. Chapman went on to say that the succeeding station captain, E. B. Cobb, then owner of the island, and a third man killed 2,800 birds in three days on and near Cobb's Island. They packed the birds in cracked ice, shipped them to New York for skinning, and were paid ten cents for each one.

In 1910, Arthur T. Wayne reported that in the Carolinas, hunters came from the north to shoot the defenseless birds and in one season killed all the breeding Least Terns on Bull's Island.

Still farther south in Florida, W. E. D. Scott (1887) described seeing hunters with Wilson's Plovers (breeding),

A Least Tern feeds its incubating mate a small fish every 20–30 minutes. In this sequence, the one doing the fishing fed its mate and was gone in 1 1/2 seconds.

Least Terns, and various kinds of sandpipers. The birds were to be skinned, partly filled with cotton, wrapped in paper, and packed away to be finished after reaching the north. The hunters Scott saw were killing 100 to 150 birds per day. Least Terns were almost eliminated from the United States but came back strongly after receiving legal protection in 1913. They are again under pressure, but this time the force is much more subtle: the destruction of prime nesting habitat by the increasing human population.

Several female Least Terns were sitting on eggs within about a 30-foot radius of me. While I watched, their mates didn't share incubation duties. The females sat on their nests the whole time while their mates flew back and forth, bringing a fish every fifteen to thirty minutes. The returning males circled 10 or 15 feet overhead, pulled up into the wind, and dropped almost vertically to land right beside their nests. I tried unsuccessfully to photograph different ones feeding their mates, then finally figured it out. In only two to three seconds he would land, give her the fish, and fly off, while she swallowed the fish. By the time I swung my camera around to photograph the feeding, he was gone. Finally I turned the motordrive on, focused on one female, and waited. Again and again the male returned to the nest with a single fish, and each time he landed, I held the shutter release down until he was gone, shooting seven to ten photographs. I shot several rolls of film, not having any idea whether I was getting anything at all. When I got the slides back, there he was giving her the fish; she swallowed it, while he went for another. Success at last.

The Corps of Engineers, in conjunction with the National Marine Fisheries, planted smooth or saltmarsh cordgrass (*Spartina alterniflora*) in the shallows behind the long, curved shell bank on Little Pelican Island, to study the effects of channels into marshes. This marsh is thriving, and now the marine biology students at Texas A&M University in Galveston are doing long-term studies to compare this human-made marsh with an adjacent natural marsh. The grass is helping to hold the bank together and, at the same time, to expand the feeding areas for the fish and birds. On the small sand flat at the very tip of this bank, one hundred Black Skimmers were nesting;

about half of the newly dug depressions had eggs. Forster's Terns were nesting in the edge of the grasses around the skimmers' nests. One nest had two chicks less than three days old; the rest had eggs. One of the down-covered siblings walked away from its nest and tried to find shade under my heel. Luckily, I saw it coming and returned it to its nest.

Along the western shell bank the Royal and Sandwich terns, nesting in "cacophonies" of one hundred to four thousand, were scattered along the shell bank and sand flats for about 800 yards. The noise was absolutely deafening. They prefer togetherness, allowing just enough room between nests to land and take off, spending their days fussing with and squawking at their neighbors while caring for their eggs. During the cool of the night they incubate their eggs; during the day they alternate between incubating them and shading them from the blistering sun, occasionally turning the eggs with their beaks. Another two thousand had joined the colony since I was here in late April, and they all had eggs, one per nest. The Sandwich Terns' nests average 15 inches apart; the Royals spread theirs out to about 18 inches.

A new Black Skimmer colony had been established on the shell bank between two tern colonies since my last trip to the island. I saw scrapes in the sand but no eggs until I wandered farther on and found one nest with three eggs.

A Black Skimmer returned from feeding with a fish that was apparently dead because it looked rotten and was falling apart. The bird was chewing or gumming (perhaps we should say "beaking") the fish and repeatedly dropping it in the shell. A complete mess, the fish was softened to the point of falling apart, and completely coated with sand and broken shell. The skimmer tried to swallow it tail-first several times, then finally got it turned the right way and succeeded. Skimmers are certainly less aggressive than the gulls. Through the whole process, none of the neighboring skimmers tried to steal the fish.

All the Laughing Gull nests I saw had one to three eggs each. Out on the sand flats there were six Royal Tern nests with eggs, the smallest group I had ever seen. An earlier group of about one hundred was nesting inland. Half of the eggs had hatched within the last few days, and the rest were on the verge of hatching. I was standing 40 yards off, watching through my binoculars. The temperature was going to be 90° F, and the parents were standing over the nests shading the chicks and eggs from the early summer sun. Some parents brought fish back to the nestlings, but the chicks were more interested in staying in the shade than feeding, and I could see sand flying as the youngsters tried to burrow under their parents. Even though I was standing well away from the colony and most of the birds were settled down, there were two to three self-appointed guardians who didn't like my presence and were swooping and squawking at me.

Black Skimmer

Rynchops niger
FAMILY: LARIDAE

This Black Skimmer is incubating its eggs in a colony on Little Pelican Island.

Rynchops is a joining of the Greek *rhynchas,* "beak," and *ops,* "face," to mean "beak-faced," in reference to the long, razor-like bill. The species name *niger* is Latin for "black" and refers to the plumage. The common name, Black Skimmer, was given by Pennant in 1773. This skimmer has also been known as the cut-water, knifebill, scissorbill, sea-dog, shearwater, storm gull, and flood gull. The skimmer is the only bird with a longer lower mandible than upper.

With its long, thin wings, white face, white underparts and black upperparts, and long red bill, the Black Skimmer is seldom confused with any other bird. In the United States Black Skimmers nest in southern California, along the Atlantic Coast from Massachusetts south to Florida, and all along the Gulf Coast. They also breed on both coasts of Mexico south to southern South America. In the winter they range from southern California south to Chile on the Pacific Coast, from Virginia south to Argentina on the Atlantic, and on the northern Gulf Coast. Before the coasts became so populated, the skimmers nested on the beaches above the high tide mark. The presence of people drove them to the spoil islands in the bays.

The always gregarious skimmers nest out on the open sand flats and shell banks next to but not necessarily mingling with Laughing Gulls and Royal and Sandwich terns, although Forster's or Gull-billed terns sometimes nest with the skimmers. Black Skimmers always sit on their nests facing into the wind. When disturbed, they all rise and take to the air, circling around, protesting noisily with their peculiar yelps, flying straight toward the intruder, only veering off when they are within a few feet, then settling back down on their nests. In the days of the millinery trade, skimmer parts were used for hat decorations and their eggs were gathered for food.

The skimmer scrapes out a depression an inch or so deep, 4 to 6 inches wide, and lays two to five grayish-white mottled eggs which, against broken oyster shell, are almost invisible. Young birds, also light mottled gray, blend in with the oyster shell and freeze absolutely motionless when predators come around. After they have grown feathers but not yet fledged, they still use their ability to freeze to escape danger. The fledgling skimmer's long lower beak makes it impossible for it to pick any food off the ground, so it must either be fed by the parent or learn to feed itself by skimming. And in order to feed itself by skimming, it must be an adept flyer.

Fledging is a very precarious time for these young birds, who have to master the arts of flying and feeding themselves in a very short time. When they start flying, they don't know how to guide themselves or avoid objects. I watched one young skimmer fly into a low bush, bounce off, and tumble over backward on the ground. Others fly and land in the marsh grass, unable to take off again. I have rescued several in this situation and have always been rewarded with a peck.

Skimmers are the only birds in these colonies that do a broken wing act: they circle around, flapping weakly, and let their feet drag or their wing tips touch the water (the only time a skimmer will let this happen). Other times they will land on the shell bank, wings spread, looking helpless, giving a textbook lesson on how to distract a predator from the nest.

A skimmer brought a dead, stiff fish, curved like the new moon, to its downy chick, who grasped it in the middle. Try as it might it could not swallow the fish crossways and, after several unsuccessful tries, dropped the fish on the ground. The parent, standing patiently by, picked up the fish, tried to soften it by chewing, and gave it back to the chick. The cycle went on a dozen times. Human parents would have quickly lost patience, but not the parent skimmer. It kept repeating the process until the young bird was able to grasp the fish by the head and start the swallowing process. It was not easy for a 4-inch-long bird to swallow a stiff, 3-inch-long fish, but eventually the entire fish disappeared into the struggling young bird.

Two young Snowy Egrets have hatched, a third is on the way; the fourth will come along later.

In the bird colony there are always some dead chicks; the mortality rate is very high. For these birds to survive and flourish into the future, they will require active intervention rather than the passive unconcern we now show them. Fire ants are one serious hazard: I saw one newly hatched but nearly dead chick with ants crawling all over it. I brushed them off, but it was probably too late. The ants, looking for food, swarm into newly opened eggs and eat the chicks alive. The birds have no defense against these menacing ants. Controlling them requires treating the islands with specific fire ant insecticides, or preferably with the newer fenoxycarb (LOGIC™), very early in the spring before nesting begins and again in the late summer. The nesting success rate on the islands that have been treated, Rollover Pass and North Deer, has shown a great improvement. The small islands can be easily treated by hand, but the larger ones like Pelican Island, Little Pelican Island, or North Deer Island, with their dense vegetation, are difficult to treat.

In late May, Caspian Terns were nesting on the outer edge of the western shell bank on South Deer Island. I arrived early in the morning, set the blind in the marsh behind the shell bank, and scanned the colony through my camera lens. As soon as I got inside the blind, a parent brought a fish to one of the smallest chicks in the colony. The scene was beautiful! The young bird was in full sunlight, filling my viewfinder. The parent strutted around the colony holding the 4-inch fish and finally presented the fish, headfirst, to the chick. I was as excited as the chick. These were going to be fantastic pictures! Just then the other parent stepped directly between the lens and the chick, acting as a living curtain through the whole feeding process. After the chick had swallowed as much of the fish as it could, it stepped into the open and walked around for another twenty minutes with the fish tail extending from its mouth.

Nesting was a continuing process in this colony. At the southern end some young birds were ready to fly. As I turned the lens and scanned to the north, I saw younger and younger birds, some only days out of the egg. Farther north a loose-knit group of terns sat on eggs, and beyond them were some scrapes in the shell bank for future nests.

Caspian Tern

Sterna caspia
FAMILY: LARIDAE

The species name is the feminine form of the Latin Caspius, for the Caspian Sea, where the type specimen that Pallas first described in 1770 was collected. The genus name started out as *Sterna*, was changed to *Hydroprogne*, and is now *Sterna* again. It is more consistent to place the terns in the genus *Sterna*, but *Hydroprogne*, which comes from the Greek *hydro*, "water," and from Latin Progne, Pandion's daughter, who according to legend turned into a swallow, is much more romantic. Literally, the name means "water swallow." Common names have been cayenne tern, gannet striker, striker, imperial tern, and redbill.

The heavy red bill and solid black (breeding) or streaked (winter) cap that never shows the white forehead are the most obvious markings that separate the Caspian from the Royal tern. The Caspian is the largest of the terns, being nearly as large as a Herring Gull, and has almost worldwide distribution. It is found around fresh as well as salt water and in

This Caspian Tern is making itself heard by the rest of the colony.

North America breeds on the West Coast from Baja California north to Washington, inland to Utah and Wyoming, and from Manitoba southeast to the Great Lakes and northeast to Newfoundland. It also breeds on the Atlantic Coast from Virginia south to Florida and along the Gulf Coast to Texas and Mexico. In winter it ranges from southern California, the northern Gulf of Mexico, and Florida south to Venezuela and Colombia.

Caspian Terns have never been overly abundant. They are shy and difficult to shoot, and as a result were not killed for the millinery trade, but Bent (1921) quoted W. B. Barrows, who wrote that the Caspian Tern populations on Lakes Erie, Huron, and Michigan were affected by Indians and fishermen who took the birds' eggs for food. Those northern colonies, especially in the Lake Michigan area, were severely reduced by the egg gatherers who took the gull and tern eggs not knowing (or caring) that these birds, unlike the domestic chicken, are "determinate" layers. Terns and gulls normally lay one clutch of eggs and, if these are removed or destroyed, may lay a replacement clutch, but they don't keep laying indefinitely. A chicken, on the other hand, is an "indeterminate" layer. The removal of eggs stimulates more laying.

Caspians, the least gregarious of the terns, prefer to nest apart from the other colonial birds on very small islands or isolated shell banks they can have all to themselves. When they find it necessary to nest on the larger islands, they will gather in their close-knit colonies and generally avoid mingling with the other birds. Caspian Terns adapt to the local conditions, and their nests, it is said, may be formed of moss, built on floating masses of grasses in a marsh, or lined with grasses or mosses. They are also described as laying one to four eggs in a clutch. All the nests I have seen have been simple scrapes in a shell bank and have contained only one to three eggs.

The Caspian's favorite and almost exclusive food is small fish, which it catches by diving bill-first into the water. Flying along at a low altitude with its bill pointing down, hovering occasionally to check out a fish that it has spotted, the bird plunges headfirst into the water, sometimes submerging completely, and then, wings flapping, bounces out like a cork that has been held underwater and released.

A Caspian Tern brings its chick a whole mullet. The Caspians bring sizable fish and seem to only feed 2–3 times per day.

   During the hottest part of the day, the very young birds like to burrow under their parents, who provide their only protection from the sun, wind, and rain. The fact that this reef is entirely barren is of no concern to the chicks, since all their needs are drawn from the bay: all the minerals, vitamins, protein, calcium, and moisture these little birds need are in the fish the parents bring to them. Caspians don't regurgitate for the babies, but rather bring the whole, fresh fish. The smaller Forster's Terns catch tiny fish and feed their chicks every thirty to forty-five minutes. The Caspians bring their young much larger fish and apparently feed only two or three times per day.
   One parent brought a fish back to the colony, but either it didn't find its young or the chick was not interested in feeding. After being out of water for awhile, the fish dried out, so the parent took off, circled out over the water, and dipped the fish in the water to moisten it again. It may be difficult for the chick to swallow a dried fish.
   Suddenly, all of the adults squawked and took to the air as if someone had announced a fire drill. I looked out from the blind but didn't see anything amiss. All the young birds, seeing their parents' alarm, ran to the water and swam away from the island. The parents quickly calmed down but then had the task of herding the small birds back to the island, which they did by going out to the swimmers, swooping down, and flying just over the chicks' heads in the direction of safety. Sometimes they actually hovered right over the chick. Time after time they

circled around, showing each chick the way back to the nests, taking no rest until all were safely ashore.

Peter Brown, a prominent Houston photographer, Jill, his wife, and I landed on Little Pelican Island, anchored the boat securely, and leisurely walked to the south tip of the western shell bank. Out on the open sand a colony of about one hundred Black Skimmers was well established. Sitting on some washed-in logs and watching through our binoculars, we saw some very small chicks in their nests and some larger chicks, still in down, walking around the colony. On the outer perimeter there were nests with eggs, and the latest-comers were just starting with their scrapes in the sand. In the marsh grasses edging the sand flats, there were about forty Forster's Tern nests with a fifty-fifty mix of eggs and chicks. After getting a good count of the nests and taking some pictures of the young skimmers, we walked back to a raised, grassy, prickly pear cactus area in the center of this shell bank. A colony of about four hundred Laughing Gulls claimed this area, and we took several photos of some gull chicks in nests right along the edge of the bank.

Until then the breeze had been out of the southeast at 10 to 15 knots. The wind died; then a cool, gentle breeze from the northwest quickly escalated to a storm with winds over 30 knots which swamped small boats and drowned two people in the immediate area. Waves built up, wind whipped the tops off the whitecaps, and salt spray filled the air. The boat washed in sideways on the shore and filled with water, but, with some effort, we pushed it off and towed it to sheltered water on the lee side of the shell bank. Meanwhile, waves rolled completely across the low parts of the bank. The Black Skimmer and Forster's Tern chicks and eggs we had just photographed at the south tip of the shell bank were washed away. Storms are natural hazards that these birds must face. The ground-nesting terns and skimmers sometimes select sites that are on low-lying terrain and, lacking mobility, their eggs and chicks are very vulnerable for about a two-month period. The gulls on the central part of the shell bank and the gulls, terns, and skimmers on the northern part of the shell bank were on higher ground and were not affected by the storm.

Forster's Tern

Sterna forsteri
FAMILY: LARIDAE

Forster's Tern chicks, and all other young birds, think they should be fed every time their parents come near.

Forsteri is the Latinization of the name Forster. Nuttall first recognized the Forster's Tern as being a separate species from the Common Tern and named it for the German naturalist Johann R. Forster in 1834. Audubon called the bird Havell's tern. Other names have been marsh tern and sea swallow.

The Forster's Tern is the only strictly North American bird in our colony. It is equally at home around fresh and salt water, breeding in British Columbia and Manitoba south to Colorado, Iowa, and California. On the Atlantic Coast it breeds from New York south to North Carolina and on the Gulf Coast from Alabama to Tamaulipas, Mexico. In winter it is found from the central California and Virginia coasts south to Guatemala and the Greater Antilles.

The deeply forked tail, mostly orange bill, snow-white undersides, and light gray back make the Forster's Terns relatively easy to identify. They, along with the Gull-billed Terns, truly deserve the name "marsh terns" for their habit of feeding and nesting in the fresh and salt marshes. The only foods I have seen the parent terns bring their chicks are small fish and shrimp. Other observers report these terns feeding over the marshes on dragonflies, caddis flies, floating insects, and, in the West, grasshoppers.

Forster's Terns nest in a variety of places, on shell banks, mud flats, or even drifts of dead grass debris caught in the marsh grasses completely surrounded by water. Their nests, cupped and well constructed of dead grass and twigs, are normally close to the water and are often lost to storms and high tides but are safe from predators. Forster's Terns are the only birds to have physically attacked me, diving down from behind, pecking me on the head, drawing blood several times. Some might say "Good for them." I learned to wear a loose-fitting hat and carry my tripod over my shoulder so that it was the highest point.

The Forster's long, pointed wing and tail feathers were once prized adornments on women's hats. A peculiar trait of the Forster's and Least terns led to their destruction by the plume hunters in the late nineteenth and early twentieth centuries. When one was shot and fell, the other terns in the vicinity would be attracted to the fallen one. They would hover around, and one by one fall prey to the plumer's guns. When the gunners found a flock but had difficulty shooting the first one, they would tie a handkerchief to a stick and throw it into the air. From a distance this looked enough like a falling tern that the flock would fly to its destruction.

Two days later I returned to Little Pelican Island to observe the effects of the storm. All the Black Skimmer and Forster's Tern nests on the south tip of the western shell bank that we had photographed and counted had been washed over. It was a most depressing sight—nests washed away, cold eggs scattered randomly around, drowned chicks caught in the marsh grass. Depressions remained where the nests had been, but they were empty.

Immediately after the storm the adult birds regrouped back in the locations where their nests had been and started over again. Fresh scrapes appeared, new eggs were laid, and by mid-June the effects of the storm were barely discernible.

A fledgling Forster's Tern that had survived the storm flew out over the marsh and seemed to be doing very well. Ten to twenty percent of the Laughing Gull eggs on this shoreline had hatched. I stopped to photograph one just coming out of its shell. The parents offered no help as the little wet thing pushed and fought to free itself, collapsing in total exhaustion, only to rise again and continue the struggle to live.

Oh, to go back to the days of June,
Just to be young and alive again,
Hearken again to the mad sweet tune
Birds were singing with might and main.
(LOUISE C. MOULTON, "BALLADE OF WINTER")

Feeding Chicks:
The Dispersion Begins

JUNE

The birds' nesting season reaches its crescendo in the first part
of June. Activity in the colony is at its peak as eggs are being
incubated, young birds are being fed, and parents are traveling back and forth to feeding grounds to satisfy the hunger
of growing chicks. Young birds will be trying their wings,
answering their basic instinct to fly. Even in June, some latecomers will just be establishing nests, but by the end of the
month, the nesting season will be ending as the dispersal of the
early nesters accelerates.

Out on Redfish Island, the tiny Least Terns, being about
the size of large sparrows, looked much too delicate for this
harsh environment. Forty nests were hidden among the large
oyster shells on the north end of this lonely stretch of reef.
These shells were too large for the birds to move, so they found
small openings or natural depressions 10 to 20 feet apart in
which to deposit their eggs. The eggs and young were small
and difficult to see, so I didn't walk through the colony but
instead found a spot just outside from which to observe and
photograph. When I first approached the colony, I didn't see
anything moving, so I found a board, sat down, and in just a
few minutes saw small birds moving around. I was closer to
the edge of the colony than I had thought. One bird, carrying

Opposite page:
What seems to be a look
of complete adoration
by this Laughing Gull
chick is in fact an act
of begging for food.

a fish, came back, landed within 10 feet of me, found its chick, and fed it. This was too close for me to photograph with my 600-millimeter lens; any movement on my part would frighten it away, so I just sat and watched.

I finished photographing on the reefs and moved to North Deer Island for a late afternoon survey. This was the peak period of the nesting season when one can fully realize just how strung out and intertwined the nesting season is. While the earliest nesters had chicks ready to fly, late arrivals of the same species were just establishing nests and laying eggs. Some White Ibis chicks were starting to fly, and I saw two young Roseate Spoonbills, along with nine adults, flying overhead in V formation. The early nesting Laughing Gulls had almost-flying chicks, while the late ones were sitting on eggs.

In some chest-high brush some Cattle Egrets were nesting with Tricolored Herons and Snowy Egrets. Cattle Egrets are primarily inland birds, but each year five hundred to two thousand nest on North Deer Island. One, in full breeding plumage, must have had eggs or chicks in its nest in a bush at the edge of a marsh, because it was concerned about my presence. I never saw the nest, but the egret perched on the top of a bush within about 25 feet of me and displayed its plumage while I shot several photographs. When finished, I quietly backed away so it could return to its parenting duties.

At the end of the day I was walking down the shell bank, carrying all my gear, when I came upon a 4-foot Western diamondback rattlesnake looking very much out of place here on the bare oyster shell where I always anchor the boat. I stepped back, put a short lens on the camera, lay down on the shell to be on its level, and tried to photograph it. For all its reputation, the snake wouldn't coil or look fierce or anything; it just wanted to go off in the deep grass to hide. Of the islands where I photograph, North Deer Island is the only one on which I have seen snakes, these being king snakes and rattle-snakes. These snakes probably take some eggs and young birds, but if so, their predation rate must be very low because they don't seem to bother the birds. Mice and rats, which abound on the larger islands and are serious egg predators, are more likely the snakes' primary source of food. So on balance, the snakes are probably beneficial to the colony.

Cattle Egret

Bubulcus ibis
FAMILY: ARDEIDAE

The genus name *Bubulcus* is taken from the Latin *bubulus,* "of or pertaining to cattle." Previously, the name was *Ardeola ibis, ardeola* being the diminutive of *ardea,* which is Latin for "heron." Other common names have included buff-backed heron and cattle heron.

The Cattle Egret was originally an Old World species but now inhabits all the land masses except Greenland and Antarctica. It was first reported in South America in the late 1880's and again in 1911 or 1912. The first United States sighting was in Florida in 1941 or 1942 and the first recorded nesting at Lake Okeechobee, Florida, in May 1953. The first recorded nesting in Texas was in 1958. Since then the species has spread across the United States and into Canada. How it traveled from Africa to South America is unknown.

Young Cattle Egrets eagerly await the return of their parents.

The Cattle Egret is a small, white, stocky heron with a short yellow bill. In its breeding season it acquires a buff-colored crown and breast. It is not a wading bird and does not feed on marine life as its relatives do but prefers the insects flushed by the cattle and other large animals with which it associates. Along the coast it often returns to water for nesting, joining the other herons and egrets in the large colonial gatherings on the coastal islands. Inland, it will nest around lakes or ponds or in groves of trees well away from water. It adapts readily to its surroundings and builds its nest in whatever kind of tree or bush is available, whether 1 or 50 feet off the ground. The nest is a primitive twig platform 12 to 18 inches across.

The Cattle Egret seems to be capitalizing on human modifications of the environment, thriving and expanding when many of the other water birds are just holding their own. Oberholser's *Bird Life of Texas* says that we created a paradise for the Cattle Egret in the clear-cut forests, irrigated fields, and pastures. Ranchers don't risk poisoning their cattle by spraying their fields, so from year to year there is a stable and abundant supply of insects for these small egrets to thrive on.

Two days later I went to Rollover Pass to check some of the low-lying nesting areas. The violent storm six days earlier had been followed by two days of gusty winds from the south, up to 30 miles per hour, which blew in some high tides. Nests on some of the lower, more exposed islands were washed away, but here on higher ground at Rollover Pass none were affected.

It was a normal June day with a temperature of about 90° F. The wind was calm. Normal Gulf Coast humidity makes the atmosphere feel very heavy. Young Great Blue Herons were sitting on their nests panting. The parent Great Blue Heron stood on the edge of its nearby nest for more than $3\frac{1}{2}$ hours, shading the nestlings from the heat of the sun. The bird's wings were drooped, half spread, completely relaxed; its eyes closed as it dozed off for a little nap. Back in the shady brush the young Olivaceous Cormorants were panting; young egrets and the incubating Tricolored Herons—who were not sitting on the eggs but standing over them so the sun wouldn't bake the developing embryo—were doing the same thing. The older cormorant chicks were feathered and were trying their wings, flapping hard, putting power into their strokes to build muscles. These chicks were determined to fly and would succeed in just a few days.

Two Roseate Spoonbills, in the nearby nests, had a territorial dispute. Quietly they stood off, then as if on cue, started sparring. I heard the clacking as they thrust and parried with those ungainly bills, but there was no damage, and I'm not sure whether there was a winner.

On Down Deer Spoil Island most of the young Caspian Terns were able to fly or were close to learning, but there were still unhatched eggs to be seen. When one latecomer left its nest unguarded, a waiting Laughing Gull invaded immediately, pecking open one of the nest's two eggs. It pulled the wet, unborn chick from the egg by the head, held it for a second, then flipped it around in its beak until it was hanging, head down, by one foot. After that, with a quick toss of the head by the gull, the unborn tern was devoured.

Within minutes the parent tern landed near the nest, walked over and sat on the remaining egg. After a few seconds it stood up, backed away, looked confusedly at the nest, tried sitting again, but got up immediately, still confused. The nest just didn't feel right—something was wrong, but what? Birds' memories, however, are short, and in just a few minutes the parent settled back down to incubate and protect the remaining egg.

On a day when there was no wind at all, the water looked as if it had been oiled. From a distance the water and sky looked so much the same that, were it not for the narrow band of land on the horizon, they would have blended together and magically suspended me in space.

This day I did not photograph but just moved around to cover a large area and check some nesting sites, starting with the Least Tern colony on the north tip of Redfish Island that I had photographed in the middle of May. Then, the adult birds had been busy incubating eggs; this time there were none in sight. The colony had failed. The Black Skimmer and Forster's Tern colony was still intact but confined to a small area on the north tip. In past years this island had provided good nesting

Laughing Gulls are predators. This one opens a well advanced Caspian Tern egg, pulls the fetus out, and makes a meal of it.

for the Least Terns; in some years small colonies were established on the south end, in other years in the central part, but most years saw colonies here on the north end. Before they became overrun with people, dogs, and cats, the coastal beaches were the Least Terns' ideal nesting habitat. Now they are trying to nest on the islands, and people are running them off these as well. Because too many people think they have to tramp over, pave, mow, and litter every square inch of ground, there is little room where the animals can live their lives and thrive.

And since the island is not a sanctuary, the shell on the south part has been worn flat from too many footprints. It doesn't help either that the surrounding waters are popular fishing spots and that the island is a favorite rendezvous where the sailboat and powerboat people look for their weekend deserted-island getaway experience.

Swan Lake, like Redfish Island, is not a sanctuary but has long been a favorite nesting area for Black Skimmers and Gull-billed and Forster's terns. The mile-long shell bank protecting the Swan Lake marsh, which ten years ago was a solid buffer separating Swan Lake and its adjacent marsh from the open bay, is suffering the same fate as so many beaches around the coastline—erosion. Ten years ago a large pass at the south end and a small one at the north end channeled water in and out of the lake. At the north end on some higher ground, a large mass of prickly pear cactus annually hosted nesting herons and egrets. Black Skimmer and Forster's Tern colonies were scattered all along this bank. Now, the prickly pear is gone and portions of the bank have disappeared into the bay, allowing the waves to cut three new channels into the marsh. The opened channels are deepening, and the marsh is simply vanishing into the bay. Now the only nesting is on the remaining shell bank at the south end of the marsh.

The high, windblown tide a few days before had washed away one of the few Gull-billed Tern colonies in Galveston Bay. There were only a dozen Gull-billeds at Swan Lake, and they selected a site on the bay side of a shell bank, which turned out to be too close to the water. Some Black Skimmer nests had also been washed away, but one hundred or so still had active nests. A few Forster's Tern's nests had washed away, but most of them were on the back side of the shell bank and in the edge of the marsh. There were thirty-five Forster's nests, and I saw some newly hatched young.

In the central part of Little Pelican Island the wading birds were nesting in the trees and bushes. There was no way to get a good estimate of the number of birds in this jungle. Standing off, I could see the ones in exposed perches, not those down inside. There would be lots of prize-winning photographs here, but I stayed away and didn't bring people or photograph because these areas are extremely sensitive to human traffic. There is no way to get in and out without upsetting and possibly destroying nests.

Fire ants represent another threat to the birds and were well established on the island. Anytime I stopped to look at something, the first thing I did was check to see whether I was standing on a fire ant mound. These ants are well named and very aggressive. Forget just once and you will think that you are on fire.

Royal Tern

Sterna maxima
FAMILY: LARIDAE

A Royal Tern shades its newly hatched chick from the sun.

The species name *maxima* is from the Latin *maximus*, meaning "largest." *Royal* also refers to size: the species name is a misnomer, since this bird is slightly smaller and less aggressive than the Caspian Tern. Audubon and other early observers never differentiated between the Royal and Caspian terns, calling both species Cayenne terns. Other names have included gannet, gannet striker, and redbill.

The orange-red bill and white forehead (except for a brief period during breeding season) are the primary features that separate the Royal from the Caspian tern. The breeding range extends south from Maryland to central Florida on the Atlantic Coast and from northern Florida to Texas on the Gulf Coast. It also breeds on the coast of Yucatan, the Bahamas, the West Indies, and western Africa. Royal Terns winter in southern California, the northern Gulf of Mexico, and south to Argentina.

The Royal Tern is a strictly saltwater species and enjoys the company of other birds. In the breeding colonies, the Royals I have seen have always been associated with Sandwich Terns, sometimes with a few Black Skimmers and Laughing Gulls thrown in for good measure.

Royal Terns were never killed for the millinery trade, but their eggs, which are large and palatable, were collected for food. This, combined with the shooting of the other birds around them, which frightened them away, severely reduced their populations on the northern breeding grounds.

Royal Tern nests are small dug-out hollows, preferably on small coastal islands with wide-open sand flats or shell banks. The literature varies on the number of eggs in a nest—some say one to four, others one or two—but on the Gulf Coast I have never seen nests contain more than one egg. The young Royals come into the world in a variety of colors. Just-hatched chicks may be light brown or tan, dark brown, white with faint markings, or different shades of charcoal. The different colors may help each parent identify its chick.

Out on the western shell bank of Little Pelican Island, early Royal and Sandwich tern chicks had joined the crèche, which is a dense group of dependent young birds. The three hundred in one group looked to be three to four weeks old. Adult babysitters, which may or may not have been parents of the chicks they were guarding, were standing around the periphery keeping the chicks in a tight knot, making sure they didn't wander off and get lost. There are several theories of why the young birds form crèches, but the one that makes the most sense in the southern rookeries is that while the young birds are being watched by just a few adults, the other adults can spend more time feeding. About 60 percent of the Sandwich and 80 percent of the Royal tern eggs had hatched. One fully feathered Sandwich chick was standing in the crowd.

I was standing in the open, thirty to forty feet from about four thousand nesting Royal and Sandwich terns (about a fifty-fifty mix). As long as I didn't make any sudden moves, they went on with their normal routines. Thirty or thirty-five feet seems to be an acceptable range to the terns; if you come closer than that, they won't relax. With their nests always mixed in together, one would think that the species would be tolerant of each other, but I watched some spirited sparring between several incubating Sandwich and Royal terns. The Sandwiches are smaller but hold their own against the neighboring Royals. A mixed group with adults and chicks was standing around together, everyone squawking at once. One parent walked away from the group. Its chick looked a little lost for a minute, then fell in and tagged along behind. These young terns have a progression: they stay in the nest for the first few days, then hang around in mixed groups of parents and chicks, and lastly join the crèche to finish growing up with their peers.

The young Roseate Spoonbills to the right of my blind at Rollover Pass were rooster-sized and growing rapidly. In their efforts to shade themselves from the midday sun, the chicks were not staying on their nest but acting like traditional Ostriches, burrowing under the nests, shading their heads, while leaving their bodies out in the full sun. When the adults returned to the nest, the chicks forgot about the sun and besieged their parents by stretching their necks to full height and rapidly nodding their heads, occasionally pecking at the parents, trying to get the message across that they were on the verge of starvation. The chicks seemed to be saying "yes" to everything, nodding their heads up and down, up and down. Finally the parent took the hint, lowered its head, opened its beak, and let them feed.

Sandwich Tern

Sterna sandvicensis
FAMILY: LARIDAE

The species name *sandvicensis* is the Latinized form of Sandwich, for the village in Kent, England, where the first specimen was taken. Before 1983 the genus name was *Thalasseus*, which was from the Greek *thalassa*, "sea," which originally came from *hals*, "salt." The common name until 1972 was Cabot's tern; others include yellow-nibbed tern, Boy's tern, ducal tern, and Kentish tern.

The Sandwich Tern's long, slender, yellow-tipped black bill is an excellent field mark for this bird. It is a medium-sized, widely distributed uncommon tern that is restricted to salt water. In the New World it breeds from Virginia south to Florida, across the Gulf Coast, and south to Mexico and South America. In Audubon's time it was not known to breed north of Florida. In the Old World it nests in the British Isles,

During nesting season the Sandwich Terns, kept busy bringing fish back to their chicks, have the problem of picking their chicks out of several hundred in the crèche.

Denmark, Sweden, Sicily, northwest Africa, and the Black and Caspian seas. In wintertime it is found from the northern Gulf Coast and Florida south to southern Brazil and Peru.

The Sandwich Terns nest on isolated sand and shell banks in the saltwater bays and along the shores. They are very sociable birds, gathering in dense flocks at nesting time, always with the larger Royal Terns. For a nest they usually dig a shallow depression; sometimes they don't bother and just lay on the sand or shell. Bent says that Sandwich Terns normally lay two eggs. *The Birder's Handbook* says one or two eggs are usual, with three occasionally, and that the clutch size increases with age. I have never seen more than one egg per nest on the Texas coast.

The porous sand flats and shell banks of Little Pelican Island provide prime nesting sites for the Royal and Sandwich terns. When it rains, water does not accumulate in the depressions but drains quickly into the soil. If birds have the misfortune to nest in a soil containing too much clay, the depressions are slow to drain; then, upon drying, the egg sticks to the bottom and cannot be turned by the parent, and the embryo dies.

Farther to the right was a nest with two one-week-old Great Egret chicks, the larger one a day or two older than the other. At feeding time the larger chick, being the strongest, fed first, pecking at its smaller nest mate to drive it away so it could get all the food. After feeding the larger one, the parent pulled away and rested on a bush close by the nest. The larger chick was still pecking randomly at the smaller sibling, but not hurting it. As soon as the parent stepped back on the nest, it was set upon again by the chicks, the larger one leading the way. Each time the parent lowered its head, the dominant chick was the first to grasp its bill, but the parent pulled away and after several tries maneuvered the smaller chick into position to feed.

Snowy Egrets were nesting down inside and under the bushes, very difficult places to photograph. So far in its short life, the young, almost feathered Snowy Egret, perched on a branch in front of the blind, had seen only its nest and its immediate environs. Now it glimpsed a little of the world, treading through and over the bushes, getting caught in some branches, struggling, freeing itself, and continuing its walk. It tried its wings and didn't go anywhere, but a few minutes later put some power into the strokes and completed its flight from one bush top to another. While this young bird was becoming independent, an adult under another bush was in at least the second week of incubation. Snowys were feeding their chicks regularly, but I had not gotten a good look yet. The older chicks were roaming around, begging for food and, when they found their parents, going into a frenzy, flapping and squawking, literally attacking the parent. Periodically, the parent had to retreat and calm things down to bring some order to the feeding process.

Snowy Egret

Egretta thula
FAMILY: ARDEIDAE

Snowy Egrets are very restless: incubating, then standing over the eggs, then leaving to move around the colony.

The name *thula* is a Chilean name and, according to Choate (1985), was given by Molina (1740–1839), a Chilean naturalist who first described the species in 1782. Gruson, in *Words For Birds* (1972), offers another explanation: Thule was the name "given by the ancient geographers to the (unknown) north-ernmost part of the world and would appear to refer to the whiteness, as of snow."

The species was also listed as *Leucophoyx thula* (Oberhol-ser), *Ardea candidissima* (Nuttall), and *Egretta candidissima* (Bent). Common names have included short white, snowy heron, little snowy, little white egret, small white heron, little egret, lesser egret, Brewster's egret (western United States), and bonnet martyr.

The Snowy Egret has a wide nesting range: in the west in northern California, Idaho, Colorado, Arizona, and New Mexico; centrally on the Gulf Coast and in southern Oklahoma and the Mississippi Valley; in the east from Long Island south to Florida; and throughout the West Indies and Central and South America. Nests of the Snowy Egrets, loosely woven of small sticks, are small, flat platforms. They are mixed with other colonial birds' nests in low trees and bushes, and occasionally on the ground. The eggs average 43 millimeters (1.70 inches) long and are indistinguishable from the Tricolored Heron's. The only way to tell for sure is to see the bird on the nest.

Its flowing snow-white plumage, black bill and legs, and bright yellow feet make the Snowy Egret one of nature's true gems. The birds are also among the more aggressive birds in the colony, spending the day walking cockily around displaying their plumage and, like neighborhood bullies, picking adversaries and attacking with strong wing blows and rapier beaks. Encounters last only a few seconds, and there are seldom any injuries.

Called the "short white" by hunters, the Snowy Egret is tamer than the Great Egret and, as a result, suffered more from the guns of the plume hunters. Feathers of the Snowy Egret, known as "cross aigrettes" in the millinery trade, were in greater demand than those of the Great Egret because they were smaller and easier to work with. The feather merchants of the late 1800's were dealing in hundreds and thousands of pounds of feathers per year. I once found a fresh dead bird and took all the decorative feathers to a laboratory to be weighed. The feathers weighed 1.178 grams. At 28.35 grams per ounce, it would take twenty-four birds to supply one ounce of feathers.

In A. C. Bent's *Life Histories of North American Marsh Birds* (1926), there is a quotation used by the National Association of Audubon Societies in its special leaflet No. 21 for its education campaign. The paper, written by A. H. E. Mattingley of Melbourne, Australia, was originally published in *The Emu* and describes the slaughter taking place in that country to satisfy the millinery trade. Mr. Mattingley ends his description with a plea straight from his heart:

"What a sickening sight! How my heart ached for them! How could anyone but a cold-blooded callous monster destroy in this wholesale manner such beautiful birds—the embodiment of all that is pure, graceful, and good?"

Most of the Olivaceous Cormorants had left the colony for the season, but there were still eight to ten nests with young, almost grown chicks. On the boat ride to the island I passed several abandoned fishing camps that had young and adult cormorants sitting on pilings. There were also two "gulps" of cormorants sitting on the bank along the Intracoastal Waterway.

The next day, along the western shell bank of Little Pelican Island, thousands of Royal and Sandwich tern chicks were suggesting that there is some truth to the adage about finding safety in numbers. Young birds travel in dense crèches, several hundred to more than a thousand in each, which move as singular entities, always guarded by adults.

I had some success approaching the groups by standing slightly outside their critical distance until they were completely at ease, then moving a foot or two at a time, pausing to make sure I had not disturbed them. Sitting or crawling works even better because I present a smaller profile. By exercising patience I could move within 10 to 20 feet of the colony while they carried on their daily activity.

Amazingly, in all the clamor and activity, the parents search out and locate their own chicks by voice recognition. Royal Terns find their chicks by watching for recognition responses to the parent's calls. The young are willing to take food from anyone, but the adults will feed only their own. This assures

A small white-phase and two red-phase Reddish Egret chicks eagerly await the arrival of their parent, who is bringing a meal.

that all get fed and not just a few over-aggressive ones. The parents, each carrying one fish, circled around, looking for their young, dipping low over the colony, always into the wind, sometimes landing on the outskirts of the colony. If the parent found its chick on the edge of the group, it simply walked over and presented the food to it. If the adult found its chick in the midst of the crèche, it would hover overhead, and lower the food to its up-stretched beak, offering food only if it was convinced no other adult or juvenile was within range to steal it. When the parent offered food, the young bird downed it in one gulp. There is no dawdling over food in the tern colony.

About noon I moved to the permanent blind that I had erected in February in the Great Egret nesting area. To the left of the blind was a nest with three down-covered birds about two weeks old. The nest was in the top of a tall bush but was provided with enough shade that the chicks were protected from the midday sun. Two of the birds were healthy and alert.

The third was trying to hold itself erect but was too weak, a pathetic sight, dragging itself around the nest. One of the strong chicks saw the weak one move, picked it up in its beak, and shook the helpless chick like a rag doll. Not once but several times. No malice intended—just the way they do things. What can I do to help the weak bird? Nothing.

The next time I went back, there were two healthy chicks in the nest and a small, limp white body hanging on a branch under the nest.

On the next trip to Little Pelican Island I put my portable blind in a Laughing Gull nesting area near some Tricolored Herons. The herons were in brilliant breeding plumage but were not cooperating. They would show themselves partially, then disappear inside the bushes to sit on their eggs. I was more successful with the gulls. One brought a fish which was too firm for its chick to eat, so the parent reswallowed the fish to allow the powerful digestive juices to soften it somewhat. The second time up the fish was still too firm, but on the third try the fish was sufficiently softened so that while the parent held the fish, the chick could peck off enough small pieces for a meal.

In the afternoon I moved to the sand flats and set the blind near a group of seven to eight hundred Sandwich Terns that had each laid a single egg in small scrapes within 1–2 feet of each other. The noise was deafening with the constant squabbling, bickering, coming, and going. During this part of the day they stood over the eggs, shading them from the sun, letting the warm air circulate around them, periodically using their beaks to turn the eggs over to keep the embryos inside from settling to the bottom.

Through the telephoto lens I watched a Black Skimmer family with one chick and one egg in the nest. The chick was too young to endure the summer sun, so the parents took turns shading it. One would stand over the chick and egg for ten to twenty minutes, then, for no apparent reason, walk away, fly off, circle around, and land nearby. As soon as the one left, the other parent would walk up and do its duty as the provider of shade. And so it went through the day, each parent taking its turn with babysitting duties.

Tricolored Heron

Egretta tricolor
FAMILY: ARDEIDAE

A Tricolored Heron incubates its eggs in the rookery at Rollover Pass.

The species name *tricolor,* Latin for "three-colored," was adopted by the American Ornithologists' Union in 1983. The older genus name, *Hydranassa,* was much more colorful than *Egretta. Hydr* is Latinized from the Greek *hydor,* "water." *Anassa* is Greek for "queen," so that we have a mixed Greek-

Latin word meaning "water queen." The bird's former common name, Louisiana heron, was also changed in 1983. The name was given by Alexander Wilson (1766–1813) for the area covered by the Louisiana Purchase and not for the state. The bird has also been known as lady-of-the-waters, Louisiana egret, silver-gray heron, scoggin, and demoiselle.

The breeding range extends from the Chesapeake Bay south to Florida, and from the Greater Antilles south to Trinidad, as well as across the Gulf Coast, Baja California, Mexico, Central America, and South America to Ecuador and northeast Brazil. During the nesting season these herons prefer to be on or close to salt water, but after nesting they sometimes move inland to freshwater ponds and rivers. They mix their flat, loosely woven platform nests, often lined with grass and leaves, with the nests of the other colonial birds in low trees and bushes. Their pale greenish-blue eggs are indistinguishable from those of the Little Blue Herons and Snowy Egrets. Until the Cattle Egrets established themselves, the Tricoloreds were the most numerous of the herons.

With their overall slate-blue color with white foreneck and belly, the Tricolored Herons are very beautiful birds, but their feathers were never in demand in the millinery trade. As a result their populations were never decimated as were the Great and Snowy egrets.

Two Laughing Gull chicks, out for a stroll on Little Pelican Island's western shell bank, intruded into a skimmer colony, immediately provoking the adult skimmers to attack them, diving and squawking, knocking them over several times, pecking them repeatedly until the chicks could pick themselves up for a quick retreat to their own territory.

Two days later, I went to see the Laughing Gulls on Little Pelican Island. The gulls' favorite nesting areas are on sand flats or shell banks interspersed with grasses or scrubby bushes. Most nests were next to or just inside the vegetation line; others were out in the open. A typical nest is a pile of twigs and grasses laid on the ground and cupped in the center to hold two or three eggs.

Laughing Gull

Larus atricilla
FAMILY: LARIDAE

The Laughing Gull, incubating its eggs, pants to keep cool.

Larus and the family name Laridae both come from the Greek *laros* and the Latin *larus*, meaning "ravenous seabird." The species name *atricilla* is a combination of the Latin *ater, atri,* "black," and a New Latinism *cilla,* "tail," and means "black-tailed." The species was named for the immature black-tailed bird and not the white-tailed adult. It has also been called the black-headed gull.

Laughing Gulls breed for the first time in their third year. In the breeding season they acquire a solid black hood which fades to a mottled gray for the balance of the year. The Laughing Gull is primarily a coastal bird, seldom ranging very far inland. It nests along the East Coast from northern Nova

Scotia to Florida and along the Gulf Coast from Florida to Texas and on south to Yucatan.

Other than being ground nesters, gulls exhibit very little consistency in their nesting habits. Some build large stick mounds; some build just a minimum stick and grass nest; others dig a small depression in the sand or shell; still others build platform nests in the marsh grass. On some slightly higher ground in open short-grass areas, they build neatly cupped grass nests. Typical Laughing Gull eggs are olive brown with a black mottling, but they will range from a very dark brown to solid white, like hen eggs. Until the birds came under federal and state protection in 1918, gull eggs were routinely collected for food by fishermen and oystermen.

The semiprecocial chicks come out of the eggs after twenty days of incubation almost the same color as the typical eggs, olive brown with dark mottling. They are considered to be semiprecocial because even though they come out with their eyes open and are covered with down and somewhat mobile, they are still completely dependent on their parents for food.

Gulls are truly omnivorous and are probably the only water birds that have benefited from the presence of humans. In warmer weather when food is plentiful, they catch small fish, shrimp, and crabs, or follow the shrimp and fishing fleets, picking up leftovers. When they first discovered the dumps around the coastal cities, they would feed on the garbage in the winter and then move out to traditional feeding grounds as fishing improved. Now they spend more time in the dumps and are moving farther inland away from the coast. Ironically, the dumps may provide a steadier diet, as the birds feeding there raise more young per year than the birds feeding in the traditional ways.

I assembled the blind out on the shell bank, then carried it to a grassy area to stake it down. As I did, the adult gulls took flight and greeted me in their usual fashion—splat, splatter— direct hit—thank goodness for the hat. Nests in this area were simple grass-lined cups out in the open, easy to observe and photograph.

Hatchlings stay in or near their nests for their first two or three weeks, taking refuge in the surrounding grasses when danger approaches. The chicks explore their immediate surroundings while still in down and by fledgling time are completely independent of the nest. Somehow the parent finds its wandering chick when feeding time comes. The logical progression would be for the parents to feed the young chicks soft, predigested food and the larger chicks more solid food, but gulls are not logical. Just outside the blind, not 6 feet away, one gull brought its three-or-four-day-old nestling a large, fresh shrimp. The chick pecked at it, eventually getting a few bites, but could not possibly swallow the whole thing. About 15 feet to my left another parent was regurgitating a predigested mess for its almost grown, fully feathered chick. Later, another parent brought a small fish for its offspring. It tried to feed the chick out in the open, but other adults aggressively tried to steal the fish. Finally, the parent led the chick into some deep grass to complete the feeding in private. Adult gulls will steal food right out of a nestling's mouth.

Each year in the first two weeks of June, Elric McHenry and I take part in the Texas Colonial Waterbird Census. In this survey a census is taken of all the fish-eating birds nesting in the coastal and inland colonies. All the data are collected and compiled by the Texas Colonial Waterbird Society, so that the Society, Texas Parks and Wildlife, and anyone who wishes can keep track of year-to-year population changes and the long-term trends. Together, we counted the nesting water bird populations on Little Pelican Island, Redfish Island and the other islands in the immediate vicinity, including the Swan Lake area. On these counts, we have to thoroughly walk the islands to try to get good estimates of the numbers of all the species.

The total bird population on Little Pelican Island was increasing, possibly because the salt cedars in the central part of the island were providing secure nesting for the wading birds, and the gulls and terns were finding good nesting along the wide, western shell bank. Redfish Island and Swan Lake were not doing as well.

For 1990, the final population count in our area was:

Olivaceous Cormorant	40
Great Blue Heron	70
Great Egret	120
Snowy Egret	105
Tricolored Heron	295
Reddish Egret	6
Cattle Egret	50
Black-crowned Night-Heron	253
White Ibis	150
White-faced Ibis	250
Roseate Spoonbill	100
Laughing Gull	4,030
Caspian Tern	34
Royal Tern	5,500
Sandwich Tern	7,250
Forster's Tern	1,177
Least Tern	50
Black Skimmer	337
Total	**19,917**

During one count, we found a Great Blue Heron nest with four eggs and an almost naked chick, just a few hours old, lying there with its eyes closed, too weak to raise its head, recovering from the ordeal of escaping from its eggshell prison. It was hard to believe this was going to grow up to be the most majestic of all the birds nesting here.

In Moses Lake, we visited a small island inhabited only by Forster's Terns and went ashore to count the number of nests and guess at the number of birds. Most of the eggs had hatched, and all the young birds were wearing coats of down. As soon as we started walking around the island, the young birds took to the water and started swimming downwind away from the island. By the time we got back to the boat, the little birds were in a loose-knit group 100 to 200 yards off shore. The water was choppy enough so that from the little birds' low vantage point they probably couldn't see the island. We wondered how they were going to get back to the island, so we lifted the anchor, let the boat drift out, reset the anchor, and watched. All this time the parent birds had been circling around watching the whole show, knowing where all the young birds were. As soon as we were at a safe distance, they started swooping down just over the young birds' heads, just as the Caspian Terns had done, flying slowly in the direction of the island, sometimes hovering right overhead, then circling around again. They guided all the young birds safely back to the island before they were willing to settle back down to their normal routine.

When we started doing the counts in the late 1970's, there would be five hundred Black Skimmer and two hundred Forster's Tern nests scattered along the Swan Lake shell bank. Now, with the shell bank severely eroded, there were only forty Black Skimmer nests and twenty-five Forster's Tern nests. Most nests had eggs and some had young birds. Two young Forster's Terns were fully feathered and almost ready to fledge. There had been some Gull-billed Terns, but since their nests had been washed away, they were not counted.

As we counted nests, Elric and I walked along the shoreline with our heads down, watching our footing, sometimes walking on the shell and other times wading through the marsh grass around nesting areas to avoid stepping on nests and young birds. Suddenly Elric said, "What's wrong with that spoonbill?" I looked up to see a Roseate Spoonbill standing motionless on the edge of the bank about 20 yards ahead, its back to us, its head down and its shoulders drooped like someone totally defeated, as if it was dying. I had moved to within 6 feet when it turned, saw me, and tried to escape into the water. It was tangled in something, so entangled that, thankfully, the chase was very short. I caught the bird and, holding its wings, we saw that its problem was the result of another fisher's unconcern. Monofilament fishing line was wrapped around its feet and one wing, and, in its efforts to free itself, it had tied two half-hitches around its lower bill. Fortunately, there were no broken bones or other injuries. Elric held the bird while I untied and cut the line. We finally freed the bird from its bonds and released its wings so it could take flight. The first few wingbeats were shaky and unsure, but it quickly gained strength and altitude and confidence. As we watched it fly out of sight, we felt fairly certain we had gotten to it in time.

*As soon as the adult
Brown Pelican returns
to its nest from fishing,
it is set upon by its
offspring, who wants
to be fed immediately.*

The next day, I went back to South Bird Island in Laguna
Madre to see the only American White Pelican nesting area on
the Gulf Coast, with Ray Little, ace Audubon warden, as my
guide. Young pelicans grow at a phenomenal rate, reaching full
size and flying in just over two months. Some of the older
young birds were growing their primary wing feathers and
looked to be about three weeks away from flying. Late-nesting
adults were still sitting on eggs. Nesting season here extends
from late April into August, and eggs are laid from the first of
May to the middle of July. When we arrived at the island, we

anchored out and waded around the island, well away so we didn't disturb the birds. Two pods of half-grown chicks were walking and wading around on the east side of the island. They didn't know what to make of me at first and were a little wary, but by standing, moving a few feet, being very patient, I was able to get some photographs without upsetting them. All the young birds looked well fed, but I didn't see any feeding.

In Corpus Christi Bay, the young Brown Pelicans were growing fast. A few brown-headed fledglings had already joined the flock and were standing along the shoreline with the adults, the positive results of some early nesters. Brown Pelicans lay eggs from the first of April to the first of July, so while the earliest chicks had fledged, some adults were sitting on eggs. This island is an NAS sanctuary, so I didn't set foot on land but rather stayed well away and scanned the colony with my 800-millimeter lens. I could see young birds of all sizes and ages and watched four parents feed their chicks. Young pelicans are just as insistent about feeding as young cormorants. When the parent lands on the nest, it is savagely set upon by the "starving" nestlings. To get some peace and quiet while the chicks' food digests, the parents would retire to some nearby bushes. Brown Pelicans seem to feed randomly throughout the day. In two visits I did not see the white pelicans feed their young. I suspect they prefer feeding in the mornings and evenings.

Back on North Deer Island a Great Blue Heron returned to its nest and three very excited, almost grown youngsters. With the parent's arrival, the young birds became extremely animated, flapping their wings, making their guttural noises, pecking at the parent and each other. Finally, after a short wrestling match, the parent regurgitated three 1-foot-long fish that, upon hitting the nest, were snapped up and swallowed whole by the young birds. Lunch was over in just two seconds.

Some of the young Olivaceous Cormorants were fully feathered and flying; others would be flying within a week or two. From the top of the northernmost hilltop, I could survey about sixty cormorant nests, and all the juvenile birds I saw were flying or just on the verge. I watched several young birds exercise their flight muscles, building their strength, flapping mightily but not going anywhere. Fledglings start with short flights from one branch to another right around their nest. As their confidence and strength increase, flights range out to the next tree, and so on. Those that survive the transition to adulthood take their place in the "gulp."

White-faced Ibis

Plegadis chihi
FAMILY: THRESKIORNITHIDAE

The genus name *Plegadis* is taken from *plegas,* which in Greek means "scythe" or "sickle" and refers to the bill. The family name comes from the Greek *threskera,* "religious worship"

A White-faced Ibis walks by in the marsh looking for worms and insects. Its offspring, in the background, is practicing foraging for itself.

or "sacred," and *ornis* or *ornithos*, "bird." The species name *chihi* may be the name given to the bird by South American natives. The ibises were considered sacred in ancient Egypt, and the name *ibis* is carried over from the Egyptian name to both Latin and Greek. The Egyptian god of learning, Thoth, had an ibis head.

In the Life Histories series by A. C. Bent, the bird is known as the White-faced Glossy Ibis, *Plegadis guarauna.* The Limpkin, *Aramus guarauna,* shares the species name of *guarauna,* which was the Brazilian Indians' name for the birds. Apparently the Indians did not differentiate between the Limpkin and the White-faced Ibis. The latter was known as the bronze ibis in Texas and the black curlew in California. This ibis was given its common name for its least conspicuous field marking, the thin band of white feathers outlining its face.

The White-faced Ibis breeds sporadically from Minnesota west to Oregon, south to California, Utah, Nebraska, coastal Texas and Louisiana, and farther south to Brazil, Argentina, and Chile. It prefers freshwater marshes and irrigated rice fields. Rice farmers called the ibises, herons, and egrets "levee walkers" for their habit of walking the levees and eating the crawfish which burrow holes in the dikes. Unfortunately, the rice farmers repaid this service with heavy applications of pesticides which impeded the ibis's ability to reproduce. As a result, the North American population may be declining.

In flight, the White-faced Ibis appears to be black, but up close the bird is a beautiful iridescent bronze. It can be seen flying over the marshes in long diagonal lines or in V formations. Flight is strong and deliberate: it seems to know where it wants to go and wastes no time getting there.

White-faced Ibises sometimes nest with Tricolored Herons in the low, scrubby bushes around the marsh, sometimes in loose colonies on platform nests in the deep marsh grass. When built in the bushes, their grass-lined stick nests are slightly cupped and more carefully constructed than those of the neighboring Tricolored Herons. Platform nests in the marsh are made of local reeds and grasses. New-born birds stay on the nest, but as they get older, they move freely around the surrounding territory. During the hot summer days they can be found resting in the shade under the nest. Whether they are on the nest or moving around the vicinity of the nest, the parents will find and feed them.

Once, as I was in my blind photographing terns out on the sand flats of Little Pelican Island, I felt something tugging at one of my pants legs, looked down, and saw a young White-faced Ibis nibbling at it. The ibis was strolling around the nesting area and had found an opening into my blind. Apparently, it had seen my pants move and thought they must be something good to eat. I put it on my knee, where it stood completely relaxed and trusting. Needless to say, it served as a semi-reluctant photographic model before continuing its wanderings.

I had stopped by Little Pelican Island in the evening of the previous day and set up a portable blind in the marsh on the south side of the island near several of the 120 White-faced Ibis nests scattered throughout this area. From the boat I surveyed the marsh with my binoculars and didn't see very much, maybe a half-dozen ibises, but when I landed, the Laughing Gulls sounded the alarm and numerous dark heads with long, decurved bills popped up. Intermingled with the ibises and on the sand flats were 3,000 gulls. To reduce the gull predation I stayed away from this area until most of the ibis eggs had hatched. When the birds are scared off their nests, gulls and Great-tailed Grackles move right in and destroy the eggs. Some natural predation exists; the ibises don't guard their nests every minute, but I didn't want to contribute to it. The success ratio of the ibis nests seemed to be satisfactory in spite of the predators.

Here in the marsh the ibis had built platform nests using the local grasses and a few twigs. The nest right in front and closest to the blind had three chicks, two of which looked about $1\frac{1}{2}$ weeks old, the smaller, maybe 1 week. The parent had been on the nest for fifteen to twenty minutes feeding the larger two, but not the smaller one, which nonetheless looked well fed. The parent was trying to reach down to feed it, but the two larger chicks dominated the feeding. Several times the smallest chick tried to get in on the action, but failed and retired to the background.

Roseate Spoonbills don't develop the full adult coloring until their third year.

The blind was about 25 feet from the nest, closer than I realized. As I got into it, the parents flew off to a safe distance, but were back on the nests within twenty minutes. The gulls' nests were even closer, but they will sit on a nest within 5 feet of the blind. During the hot part of the day there was not much feeding. The gulls just stood around panting, and the young ibises stepped off the nests and found shade in the deep grasses.

A gull brought a fish back to its one-third grown, partially feathered chicks. The fish, very fresh, was too large for either of the chicks to swallow, and they could only try to peck off pieces. One chick attempted several times unsuccessfully to swallow it and dropped it back into the nest. Three grown gulls saw the loose fish, swooped down, and fought over it until the victor carried it away.

I left my blind up in the White-faced Ibis nesting area in the marsh on Little Pelican Island for another night. The ibis nest that had had three chicks the day before now had only the two larger ones. It's the old story of survival of the strongest. In human terms, the really sad thing is that the loss of the third chick goes unnoticed. The two remaining siblings certainly don't care, and the mother is completely unconcerned. She just feeds whoever comes, whether one or three.

In the hot middle part of the day, one ibis was on her nest incubating two eggs; another had a very small chick and was standing over it shading it from the blistering sun. The ibis colony was relatively deserted, as most of the adults were off feeding. The young ones, left to fend for themselves, stayed in the grass in the shade. The ibis standing over the small chick had its feathers ruffled straight out. Birds do this in the winter to keep warm, but that's not the situation here. Rather, it looked as if the ibis had its feathers ruffled out to get some air circulating close to the skin.

In a low bush at Rollover Pass, a Reddish Egret had a nest with three greenish-blue eggs. Nearby, a half-dozen young Olivaceous Cormorants were starting to fly from bush to bush. The cormorant nests were completely white-washed and some were partially filled with rotting, regurgitated fish. Cormorants keep the foulest nests of all.

A late group of about fifty White Ibis on Little Pelican Island were just starting to nest and lay eggs in bushes next to the sand flats. Over on North Deer Island, the earlier nesting White Ibis had already raised their young and left their nests.

Walking along the shell bank I saw two dead terns, one Sandwich and one too decomposed to identify, caught in a tangle of monofilament fishing line. During the course of normal use, the line gets nicked and worn, and when this happens, many fishers take it off their reels and throw it overboard without any thought of where it may wind up. The line drifts with the currents and washes in on a shoreline, too often trapping these animals. In this case carelessness had brought horrible death to two beautiful birds.

On down the bank I found a young gull trapped in another tangle of fishing line. This time the line was wrapped around one leg, and the gull was still alive. The chick, which still looked strong and healthy, was pulling and yanking, not understanding what was holding it prisoner. I unwrapped the line from around its leg and watched it run for its nest, flapping and squawking at the top of its voice. In the future I will scout the islands before nesting begins and pick up all the six-pack rings and monofilament fishing line.

The young Roseate Spoonbills that I had watched and photographed for the past four weeks at Rollover Pass had moved off their nests to the edge of the water, taking their places in the flock with the adults. Young Snowy Egrets were out walking around, crawling through the bushes, starting to fly from bush to bush, expanding their range as they grew and gained confidence. And the young Great Blue Herons, fully feathered and almost adult-sized, were making tentative flights from bush top to bush top. Only three nests of Olivaceous Cormorants were left; the remaining chicks were adult-sized and would leave in a few days.

The Forster's Terns' eggs to the left of my blind had hatched, and the young were about a week old. Both parents shared tending: while one shaded the nestling from the sun, the other was off feeding. After twenty to forty minutes the second parent returned, with or without a fish for the chick, and babysat while its mate went fishing. Unlike the wading birds, who bring enough food each trip to feed the entire family, the terns bring only one fish per trip. If they have two or three chicks, they have to make separate trips for each one. Then comes the problem of remembering which have and which have not been fed, if they do.

Two days later I was back at Rollover Pass, trying to photograph some Tricolored Herons who were feeding their young. Their nests were on the ground and in some low scrub, not more than a foot high, around the sand flats. Even in late June some herons were still incubating eggs, but most of the chicks had hatched and looked to be about one or two weeks old. Other young herons, almost fully feathered, were walking through the grasses.

One of the Tricolored parents stood beside the nest for an hour, then stepped onto it and gently lowered its beak for the three tiny birds to grasp. The chicks pulled and tugged until the parent regurgitated several small fish onto the nest so that all could feed equally. The parent watched carefully and if there were any leftover pieces, picked them up and reswallowed them. Digesting the fish until they are fairly soft is an essential process, since the small chicks cannot peck through the scales and skin of fresh fish. When feeding was over, the parent turned its back to the sun, shading the youngsters, and rearranged the nest, taking out a stick here, placing it over there,

Great Blue Heron parents subject themselves to seemingly vicious attacks whenever they return to their nests.

moving another just a fraction. Redecorating goes on throughout the nesting season.

A young Snowy Egret was wading around the shallows practicing feeding, stabbing at various things in the water—a floating twig, a piece of grass. It must quickly learn to differentiate between these things and real food.

A young Great Egret was out exploring, learning to fly, and, not knowing any better, landed in a Laughing Gull nesting area, where it was immediately set upon by diving, swooping, squawking gulls. The young egret, looking bewildered, cowered in the grass until finally it got out of the gulls' territory, only to walk into a Forster's Tern nesting area, which was the same thing, only worse. The terns were even more aggressive than the gulls, screaming and diving within 6 inches of the baffled egret, which seemed totally confused and unable to extricate itself from the situation. The parent was of no help; the young bird had to figure this out for itself. My attention was diverted to the Tricolored Herons, and when I looked back, the young egret had escaped.

An unfortunate Forster's Tern chick paid the price for wandering too close to a Tricolored Heron's nest. Out the back window of the blind I saw the heron repeatedly picking the chick up in its beak and dropping it. For a moment the heron looked as if it was going to eat the chick, then dropped it again. I turned my camera around as quickly as I could to photograph this, and while I watched, the heron picked the chick up thirty to forty times. Later, as I packed to leave, I walked over to the heron's nest and found the dead tern chick. Cruel as it may seem, the adult heron was simply defending its own three young chicks and territory against any intruders.

The morning of a late June day was spent in the permanent blind that I had erected on Little Pelican Island in February. The young birds in the Great Egret nest around the blind were mostly feathered, but not yet flying. One pair of egrets had selected a precarious nesting site on an outer branch of a mulberry tree. Because of some high winds a few days before, the nest had fallen completely out of the tree. Fortunately, the young birds were old enough to perch and stay in the branches on the south side of the tree, as their parents continued to come back to where the nest had been to feed them—a successful nesting in spite of the poorly chosen building site.

In the afternoon I moved to Rollover Pass and set up the portable blind near a Reddish Egret nest, perched 18 inches off the ground on a small bush. The nest was empty but, judging by the parent's reluctance to leave, I knew the young had to be close by. I studied the nest through the 600-millimeter lens and saw four chicks standing on the ground in the shade of the nest.

One of the young birds came out, climbed onto the nest, tried to communicate its hunger by tentatively pecking at its parent with no success, and retired to the shade. Shortly after, the parent flew to a nearby cove, stayed about five minutes, and returned to the nest. The process was repeated several times;

the young birds begging, the parent ignoring them, flying off, and returning, the whole time reacting with apparent indifference to the chicks' needs. While these preliminaries were going on, all four chicks—three large dark ones and one much smaller white one—randomly climbed onto the nest, begged for food, or retired to the shade. The small one looked well fed, but I was curious—how did it compete for food?

At the start of the serious feeding, the three large chicks were on the nest, while the small white one stayed under the nest in the shade. The larger ones aggressively pecked at the parent, which lowered its head so they could grab its beak. The parent regurgitated one fish onto the nest, from which it was scooped up immediately. Others went straight into the beaks and down the gullets of the small birds. It was a feeding frenzy; each chick, except the small white one still hiding under the nest, tried to get all the fish. Suddenly the parent pulled away, looked around and then stepped off the nest onto the ground, lowered its head, and regurgitated several fish in front of the small white chick. So that's how it is done! All along the parent had been keeping track of who had and who had not been fed.

As I sat out in the open on the shell bank on Little Pelican Island at the end of June photographing some terns, a young, fully feathered White-faced Ibis, still with juvenile black rings around its bill, walked by, then turned around and walked back, not 15 feet away, totally unconcerned by my presence.

The earliest Royal Tern chicks were flying. A few very late Royal and Sandwich terns were sitting on their eggs. All the young Black-crowned Night-Herons were flying, and the young, almost adult-sized Great Egrets were starting to fly and move away from the nest. The flying ones were joining the "siege" out at the edge of the marsh, the last step before total independence. Ninety percent of the skimmers and eighty percent of the White-faced Ibises and Tricolored Herons had hatched. The early gulls were flying, while others were still hatching, although not many gull nests had eggs. Some late Great Blue Heron chicks were still on their nests, but most had fledged and left the island.

If the First of July be rainy weather,
  It will rain, more or less,
  for four weeks together
(FULLER, *GNOMOLOGIA*, 1732)

The Dispersion

JULY

July is the month of the great dispersion. The birds' annual reproductive cycle is coming to a close. A very few will still be nesting, but they will have a difficult time in the summer heat. Most are leaving for the year. The young herons, egrets, ibises, spoonbills, and cormorants go with their parents and probably learn where and how to feed from them. Young gulls, in juvenile plumage, will be loitering on the banks of the islands and flying with their parents, learning their feeding techniques.

At Rollover Pass, my blind was set in an open, sandy area near several Tricolored Heron nests, one with three nearly feathered chicks that made pecking motions to try to scare me. They can survive the early July sun, but when the parent returned to the nest, they preferred to stay in its shadow. The earliest-nesting herons and Great Egrets and their young left the island for the season, others were starting to fly from bush to bush and around the nesting area, but a few late arrivals were still incubating eggs. The Olivaceous Cormorants, except for one nest with young birds, had moved out for the season. All the Snowy Egrets had hatched, some just recently, while others were ready to fly.

On another nearby nest two fully feathered Tricolored Heron chicks were flying, or would be in just a few days.

Opposite page:
The remaining
Laughing Gulls
circle overhead while
protesting the presence
of intruders.

Sibling rivalry was so strong that either chick was willing to eliminate the other so it could get all the food. The two young birds suddenly started lancing at each other, gently at first, then quickly escalating tensions into a full blown fight with strong bill thrusts, flapping wings, each one looking for an opening for the kill—no mercy given and none asked. As quickly as it had started, there was a stalemate with neither bird injured; they were equally matched and neither could get the upper hand.

Hurricane season is just around the corner. The season officially starts in June, but the latter part of August and first of September are the most dangerous times. Most of the birds time their nesting so that the young birds are grown and can fend for themselves by the time hurricanes are most probable. In early July on Little Pelican Island, the early White-faced Ibises, Great Blue Herons, Great Egrets, Black-crowned Night-Herons, and Olivaceous Cormorants had left for the season, but some birds still had eggs.

A late, mixed colony of about one hundred herons, egrets, and spoonbills was in the center of the island in some dense brush. Some nests contained small chicks; others had eggs that, it was to be hoped, would hatch soon.

Over on North Deer Island, all the early White Ibises were gone now. Several mixed groups with young birds flew over, while other young ibises perched in the trees around the island. They had had a successful year.

Young Reddish Egrets were wading in the tidal pools. Fully feathered, they were flying and starting to feed themselves.

North Deer Island is the only area in this region that regularly hosts Little Blue Herons. Most are shy, but I was lucky to fill the whole camera frame with a parent bird perched on a bush. While I stood in the open, a young white bird, apparently its offspring, came up out of its nest and started begging for food. The parent, instead, gave it some rather sharp pecks around the head, forcing it to safety back down in the nest.

On Little Pelican Island the little birds were growing up; by the latter part of July, most had left for the year; the nesting season was ending. Young Roseate Spoonbills practiced feeding in shallow water, Tricolored Herons flew from limb to limb to build their strength and confidence, and the remaining Great Egret siblings were as large as their parents. Early in the season when the birds were laying and the chicks were small, the parents had a strong urge to stay on or near their nests. At that time I could sometimes sit in the open and work to within 20 to 30 feet of the adults, but not this late in the season. The young birds were growing up and the parents were getting wilder, spending less time on and maintaining the nests, which were deteriorating rapidly. Some young birds were still being fed by their parents, but most had become independent. It was not necessary to protect the chicks from the rain and summer sun or provide the parental comforting that the younger birds need. Adults stayed away from the nest for longer periods and, when danger approached, left sooner and went farther than they had at the peak of the season.

Little Blue Heron

Egretta caerulea
FAMILY: ARDEIDAE

The Little Blue Heron is white until the start of its second year, when it molts and acquires the adult blue. During the time of molting it has been called a "calico heron."

The species name *caerulea* is Latin for "blue," which is the Little Blue Heron's predominant color. Until 1983, the name was *Florida caerula,* after the state of Florida. Other common names include levee walker, blue crane, little blue crane, and little white crane (immature). Nuttall (1919) also refers to it as a blue egret.

This heron is unique in that the immature bird is completely white during its first year, but starts molting during its first February into the adult coloring with the slate-blue body and wings and dark purple head and neck. In this intermediate stage it has been called a "calico crane." Some early naturalists thought this was a dichromatic species, like the Reddish Egret, that is, one having both light and dark phases in the adult birds. We know now that all the young birds are white and there are no white adults.

Little Blue Herons are primarily inland birds, preferring freshwater habitats, but they are also found in brackish and salt-water environments. They prefer feeding on crayfish, frogs, lizards, etc., but may also feed on grasshoppers and other grassland insects. Their breeding range in the central part of the United States includes Texas, Oklahoma, Missouri, and southern Illinois, south to the Gulf of Mexico. On the East Coast they breed from Massachusetts south to Florida. They also breed in the West Indies, Mexico, and much of South America.

The plumes of the Little Blue Herons were not in demand by the milliners, so their populations did not suffer, as did those of the Great, Snowy, and Reddish egrets during the late 1800's and early 1900's. Little Blues are social birds that prefer nesting with other herons. Like some other herons, they make do with what is available for nesting materials, with the result that some nests are primitive platforms while others are large, substantial structures. Depending on habitat, they are willing to nest in bushes 2 to 4 feet off the ground, in willows around the water's edge, or in 40-foot trees well away from water. A. C. Bent (1926) claims he never found Little Blue Herons nesting near salt water: "We did not find them breeding on any of the Keys; I have never found them breeding anywhere near salt water. We found none breeding in any of the coastal rookeries in Texas, in 1923; but we found them common and breeding in the big inland rookeries of Victoria County." However, it is common to find five to ten each year in the rookeries of the Galveston Bay complex, which, of course, is salt.

Pinpointing the Little Blue Heron nest presents a problem because of its similarity to several other heron and egret nests and eggs. Also, the egg colors and sizes are so alike the only way to positively identify a nest is to see the adult bird on it. The average sizes and typical colors of some similar eggs are:

	Color	Size (mm)	Size (in.)
Little Blue Heron	Pale blue-green	43.9 × 33.5	(1.73 × 1.32)
Snowy Egret	Pale blue-green	42.9 × 32.3	(1.69 × 1.28)
Tricolored Heron	Pale green-blue	43.9 × 32.3	(1.73 × 1.28)
Cattle Egret	Light blue	44.9 × 33.0	(1.77 × 1.30)

(Harrison and Harrison in *A Field Guide to Western Birds' Nests*, 1979)

A few young Laughing Gull chicks and some freshly laid eggs remained, but most of the gulls were flying or close to fledgling. Those that were flying had taken their places in the "splatterings" with their parents, riding the air currents like professionals; they have to learn fast or they don't survive. The ones that weren't flying ran through the grass at my approach but would soon be joining the others in the air.

A late-nesting group of Black Skimmers established a colony with fresh scrapes, newly laid eggs, and downy newborn chicks lying motionless in their nests—so soft and fragile looking that it seems amazing they can survive in such a harsh environment.

One young gull took off into the wind as I approached. It flapped mightily, gained perhaps 3 feet of altitude and, after 45 seconds, landed in the precise spot from which it had taken off. Another day or two, and it would make it.

Dry August and warm
Doth harvest no harm
(THOMAS TUSSER, 1524 – 1580, "AUGUST'S HUSBANDRY")

Hurricane

AUGUST

August is the end of the nesting season, but there will still be a few nesting birds. We may see a few herons and egrets, but most have traveled many miles to new feeding grounds by now. Most of the young terns and gulls are feeding themselves and have passed the transition to independence.

August and September are the dangerous months for immature birds because these are the most probable months for hurricanes on the Gulf Coast. The last of the Royal Terns were nesting here on Little Pelican Island on the sand flats; in August, it was like nesting in a frying pan. Walking across a large, open sandy area I saw, not 4 feet in front of me, a tiny nestling, probably three or four days old, all alone in the middle of this inferno. I took one quick picture, then left the area so its parents could come back to provide it with shade. This time of year, when most of the young are flying and have joined the flock, the birds were standing around in groups of ten to fifty that changed constantly as birds took off, circled, and landed in the same or another group. A half-dozen downy young birds were staying close to the adults. Some birds came back from a successful hunt holding small fish in their beaks, hovered over a group for a minute, landed, strutted around, heads held high, then took off and went to another group.

Opposite page:
Storm clouds gather,
but this is just another
day in the birds' lives.
They will find shelter
and ride it out.

About half grown at three weeks, the young Roseate Spoonbill is growing feathers to replace its juvenile down coat.

The eye of Hurricane Alicia came ashore 20 miles west of Little Pelican Island at about 3 A.M. on August 23, 1983. Officially, weather bulletins from the day before forecast winds to 55 miles per hour and tides to 5 feet above normal, but at the last minute the storm tightened up, increased in intensity, and packed winds of 110 miles per hour that produced tides up to 10 feet above normal. The devastation was incredible—beach homes washed and blown away, hundreds of boats sunken, power lines down, trees uprooted.

A week later I returned to Little Pelican Island to survey the damage. All the marsh and low-lying areas had been washed over by the storm-driven tides. A 30-foot shrimp boat, washed into the marsh on South Deer Island, would remain there to rot into the soil. My fixed blind that was supposed to last for several years had been blown away. The nesting season was essentially over, so there were only a few drowned Laughing Gull and Royal Tern chicks in the marsh grass, probably from late nests. With my binoculars I surveyed a mixed flock of gulls, Royal and Sandwich terns, and Great Egrets out on the sand flats. It appeared that a large number of fledglings had survived the storm. I continued on around the island and to my astonishment found that the late colony of Great Egrets, Snowy Egrets, Tricolored Herons, and Roseate Spoonbills I had seen in early July in the center part of the island was still intact. The area was above the high tide level and the nests were deep inside the bushes, where they were protected from the killer winds. The parents and chicks were going on about their business as if nothing had happened.

Thirty days hath Nouember,
Aprill, June, and September,
February hath XXVIII alone,
   All the rest have XXXI.
(RICHARD GRAFTON, *CHRONICLES OF ENGLAND*, 1562)

Migration:
The Winter Season Begins

SEPTEMBER

The birds' annual breeding cycle is coming into its most inactive period. With its decline, the birds scatter out along the coastline. The terns and gulls disperse along the beaches and coastal bays. Other birds, like the Roseate Spoonbills, move into the salt marshes. Some of the egrets and herons join the spoonbills in the coastal marshes while others move inland to freshwater habitats. As the weather cools and the days shorten, many, like the Black Skimmers, will migrate to Mexico and South and Central America. Most young birds, such as the ibises, spoonbills, egrets, and gulls, will be traveling with their parents, learning where and how to feed by imitation, perfecting their techniques with practice.

During the fall and winter months the islands provide safe roosting for the winter wading birds as well as many songbirds. Herring and Ring-billed gulls are common, as are mixed flocks of Brown and American White pelicans. In mid-September I went back to Little Pelican Island for one final look for the year and anchored the boat along the southwest shell bank. The first stop was at the shell bank's base, where there had been a skimmer colony before the hurricane. Except for several dead chicks caught in the grasses, there was no indication there had been any nesting.

Opposite page:
Laughing Gulls hover
over a nesting area on
Little Pelican Island.

In spite of intense sibling rivalry, both of these young Tricolored Herons will survive because they are evenly matched.

On the north sand flats along the water's edge was a mixed flock of 1,500 Laughing Gulls and Royal Terns with eight Great Egrets and one Great Blue Heron keeping them company. About one-third of the gulls were first-year birds. Adult gulls were already sporting the mottled white winter heads.

From the sand flats I didn't see any birds in the heron and egret nesting areas, and the late colony in the central part of the island was gone. The birds were too wild to approach for any photographing. The trees, bushes, and grasses had been watered, were growing well, and were looking lush, as there were no birds to trample or whitewash them.

I waded through the brush into the salt cedars on the north and east side of the island. Trees that had been swarming with birds two months before were empty. There was one late nest with two almost-ready-to-fly Olivaceous Cormorants. A Great Egret and a Great Blue Heron, apparently with nests that had survived the storm, took off, circled around, and landed back in the same salt cedars. All the rest had left for the year. Exposed nests had been damaged or blown away by the hurricane winds; nests positioned inside the bushes and trees had survived. I counted twenty nests within a radius of 25 feet down inside one salt cedar. The nests in the more secure crotches would provide the bases for next year's nesting.

The season was over, and in spite of the storms and people, nesting for most of the birds had been successful. The Gull-billed and Least tern colonies I was watching had failed, but other colonies on the coast had survived. The birds had dispersed for the fall and winter but, in February, would be back to do it again.

Epilogue

November is a wonderful time to be out of doors on the Gulf Coast. In that delightful time between the summer heat and the cold winter rains I went back to Little Pelican Island.

A casual observer would see no evidence that this island had, just recently, been a major rookery for at least fifteen species of the colonial birds. Flowers were in bloom on the shell banks where the Royal and Sandwich terns had nested and on the sand flats where the Laughing Gulls had nested. Trees and bushes where the wading birds had nested were lush green as they put on new growth. Brown and White pelicans, along with Laughing Gulls and Royal and Caspian terns, were resting along the shell banks. When I approached, some pelicans took flight; others waddled to the water and swam a little way out, just to keep what they consider to be a safe distance between us. The terns and gulls took off and circled around to land where I had just walked.

Rains and high water had removed all the nesting depressions that had been dug by the terns and the Black Skimmers on the western shell bank. On the sand flats there were a few scattered wing and leg bones from the birds that had died; the more fragile bones had disappeared into the soil. Just inside

Opposite page:
This salt marsh, which looks barren at first, is teeming with life. Fiddler crabs feed in the marsh grass, small crustaceans and worms burrow in the mud, and minnows feed in the shallow waters. This is where young birds learn to feed themselves and become independent.

the vegetation lines were the decaying remains of the nest mounds the gulls had so painstakingly constructed last April and May. I walked into a brushy area that had been a busy White Ibis nesting place in June and had to search for the few remnants of nests remaining in the crotches of the bushes.

From Little Pelican Island, the City of Galveston and its harbor are on the eastern horizon. To the west, across the bay, is Texas City with its distinctive skyline of chemical plants and refineries. To the north is the Texas City Dike and just beyond that, the Houston Ship Channel. In the midst of all that human activity is this island wilderness. Anglers find good catches in the waters around the island; picnickers sometimes visit the shell banks. But very few people bother the birds on the shell banks and sand flats, and no one goes into the jungle in the central part of the island where the wading birds nest. This is, spring after spring, one of the most productive nesting islands on the Texas Gulf Coast. At this writing, Little Pelican Island has no official status with the National Audubon Society or any state or federal agency. With a decreasing amount of prime wildlife habitat due to an expanding human population, the constant building of new industrial and harbor facilities, and the need, every few years, to dredge the Intracoastal Waterway, Little Pelican Island must have sanctuary status. Little Pelican Island, along with nearby North Deer Island, an NAS sanctuary, can provide some safety and security for the birds in the midst of the Galveston, Texas City, and Houston metropolitan area.

I spent most of the day on the island taking some photographs, watching the birds, and just enjoying being in this wilderness. In the late afternoon, I idled the boat away from the island, looked back, and reaffirmed my belief that this place belongs to the birds. We humans are the intruders.

Opposite page:
*This first year
Great Blue Heron
has survived the
transition from
chick to adulthood.*

Nesting Colonial Waterbird Species

Kingdom	Phylum	Subphylum	Class	Order

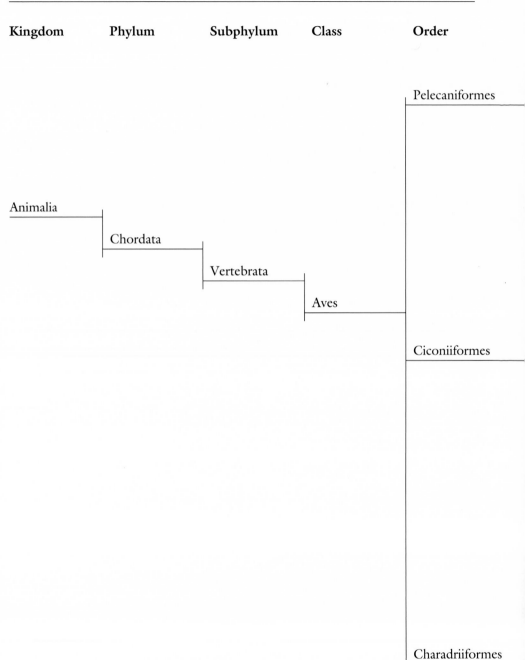

Pelecaniformes

Animalia

Chordata

Vertebrata

Aves

Ciconiiformes

Charadriiformes

Family	Genus	Species	Common Name
Pelecanidae	Pelecanus	erythrorhynchos	American White Pelican
		occidentalis	Brown Pelican
Phalacrocoracidae	Phalacrocorax	olivaceus	Olivaceous Cormorant
Ardeidae	Ardea	herodias	Great Blue Heron
	Casmerodius	albus	Great Egret
	Egretta	thula	Snowy Egret
		caerulea	Little Blue Heron
		tricolor	Tricolored heron
		rufescens	Reddish Egret
	Bubulcus	ibis	Cattle Egret
	Nycticorax	nycticorax	Black-crowned Night-Heron
	Nyctanassa	violacea	Yellow-crowned Night-Heron
Threskiornithidae	Eudocimus	albus	White Ibis
	Plegadis	chihi	White-faced Ibis
	Ajaia	ajaja	Roseate Spoonbill
Laridae	Larus	atricilla	Laughing Gull
	Sterna	nilotica	Gull-billed Tern
		caspia	Caspian Tern
		maxima	Royal Tern
		sandvicensis	Sandwich Tern
		forsteri	Forster's Tern
		antillarum	Least Tern
	Rynchops	niger	Black Skimmer

Bibliography

Bent, A. C. 1921. *Life Histories of North American Gulls and Terns.* U.S. National Museum Bulletin no. 113. Washington, D.C.

———. 1922. *Life Histories of North American Petrels and Pelicans and Their Allies.* U.S. National Museum Bulletin no. 121. Washington, D.C.

———. 1926. *Life Histories of North American Marsh Birds.* U.S. National Museum Bulletin no. 135. Washington, D.C.

Choate, E. A. 1985. *The Dictionary of American Bird Names.* Boston: Harvard Common Press.

DeBenedictis, Paul A. 1990. *ABA Checklist: Birds of the Continental United States and Canada.* Colorado Springs: American Birding Association.

———. "Coming! A New Official Checklist of North American Birds—a Revolution in Avian Nomenclature." *American Birds* 37, no. 1 (1983): 3–8.

Ehrlich, P. R., D. S. Dobkin, and D. Wheye. 1988. *The Birder's Handbook.* New York: Simon and Schuster.

Farrand, J., Jr., ed. 1983. *The Audubon Society Master Guide to Birding.* vol. 1, *Loons to Sandpipers;* vol. 2, *Gulls to Dippers.* New York: Alfred A. Knopf.

Gruson, E. S. 1972. *Words For Birds.* New York: Quadrangle/The New York Times Book Co., Inc.

Harrison, Hal H., and Mada Harrison. 1979. *A Field Guide to Western Birds' Nests.* Boston: Houghton Mifflin Co.

Lipton, James. 1968. *An Exaltation of Larks*. New York: Grossman Publishers.

Nuttall, T. 1919. *A Popular Handbook of the Birds of the United States and Canada*. Boston: Little, Brown and Co.

Oberholser, H. C. 1974. *The Bird Life of Texas*. Austin: University of Texas Press.

Pearson, T. G., ed. 1936. *Birds of America*. Garden City, N.Y.: Garden City Publishing Co.

Terres, John K. 1980. *The Audubon Society Encyclopedia of North American Birds*. New York: Alfred A. Knopf.

Texas Colonial Waterbird Society. 1982. *An Atlas and Census of Texas Waterbird Colonies*. Caesar Kleberg Wildlife Research Institute.

Truslow, Fredrick Kent. 1979. *The Nesting Season*. New York: Viking Press.

Some other field guides that may be of interest to the reader are:

The Audubon Society Field Guide to North American Birds: Eastern Region, by John Bull and John Farrand, Jr. New York: Alfred A. Knopf.

The Audubon Society Field Guide to North American Birds: Western Region, by Miklos D. F. Udvardy. New York: Alfred A. Knopf.

A Field Guide to the Birds of Eastern and Central North America, by Roger Tory Peterson. Boston: Houghton Mifflin Co.

A Field Guide to the Birds of Texas, by Roger Tory Peterson. Boston: Houghton Mifflin Co.

A Field Guide to Western Birds, by Roger Tory Peterson. Boston: Houghton Mifflin Co.

A Guide to Field Identification of North American Birds, by Chandler Robbins, Bertel Bruun, Herbert Zim, and Arthur Singer. New York: Golden Press.

Index